Celtic Mythology

Captivating Celtic Myths of Celtic Gods, Goddesses, Heroes and Legendary Creatures

Free Bonus from Captivating History
(Available for a Limited time)

Hi History Lovers!

Now you have a chance to join our exclusive history list so you can get your first history ebook for free as well as discounts and a potential to get more history books for free! Simply visit the link below to join.

Captivatinghistory.com/ebook

Also, make sure to follow us on:

Twitter: @Captivhistory

Facebook: Captivating History:@captivatinghistory

Contents

Introduction

Giants and fairies, druidical magic, impossible deeds done by heroes: all of these are features of Celtic myths and legends. Stories such as these are all that remain of the mythos of the ancient Celts, a people whose language and culture once covered a wide swath of continental Europe and extended into Ireland, Scotland, England, and Wales. However, Celtic culture and language diminished under the expansion of the Roman Empire and the advent of Christianity; its decline was well advanced by the early Middle Ages. Today, what remains of Celtic cultures may largely be found only in Brittany in northwestern France, and in Ireland, Scotland, and Wales.

We have no ancient sources for the stories of the Celts, which originally were passed down orally. Irish monks wrote versions of their native tales starting in the eighth century, while the Welsh redactions survive in manuscripts dating from the twelfth century onwards, and Cornish legends were never captured at all. Breton tales were written down even later, in close to modern times: the *Barzazh Breiz*, a collection of Breton folk songs that includes the story of the drowned City of Ys, was first published in 1839, leading to some controversy over their authenticity as representatives of ancient Breton myth and legend.

The impact first of Romanization and then the advent of Christianity on the transmission of these tales cannot be underestimated. The imposition of a new culture and new religion resulted in the loss of the original Celtic mythos, including any cosmological narratives. We now find only echoes of this original mythos in physical artefacts such as the Gundestrup Cauldron, or Neolithic tomb carvings; in the few descriptions of the Celts and their beliefs from Roman sources; or in stories such as the Irish tales of the Tuatha De Danann, or simply the Tuatha De ("people of the goddess Danu" and "tribe of the gods," respectively), who are extraordinarily beautiful, gifted warriors, learned in magic and near-immortal.

When they were finally recorded by Christian scribes, the original myths became watered down as some of the old gods were turned into superhuman heroes, while others were banished to their mounds in a mysterious and perilous Otherworld, the land of Faerie. The latter is in fact a reimagining of the function of mounded tombs made in ancient times, which kept their association with the pagan gods through their transformation into the homes of the *Sidhe*, or fairy-folk. These once-powerful beings are sometimes even further diminished when they are seen as magical, small winged creatures, the fairies and pixies who play pranks on clumsy humans.

The stamp of Christianity on the Celtic mythos can be seen in Ireland, particularly, where monks concocted pseudo-histories and linked these to Biblical tales, partly in an attempt to reconcile the ancient pagan stories with the new Christian faith. They did this, for example, by making the old gods in their guise as the Tuatha De one of several groups who invade Ireland and take up residence there, but only centuries after the granddaughter of Noah leads a group of her own people there from Palestine in an attempt to escape the Flood. Irish scribes also attempted to further valorize these pseudo-histories by claiming Irish connections to ancient Greece, in much the same way as the Romans had tried to boost their own legitimacy by claiming descent from the hero Aeneas after the fall of Troy. In these instances, exiles from Ireland go to Greece for a time where they grow strong and sometimes acquire magical learning (part of the history of the Tuatha De) before returning to Ireland once again.

Modern scholars have grouped Irish myths into one of three basic cycles: the Mythological Cycle, which contains the pseudo-histories and stories of god-heroes such as Lug and Lir; the Ulster Cycle, which contains the epic Tain Bo Cuailgne ("Cattle Raid of Cooley") and the Cuchulainn legends; and the Fenian Cycle, which tells the stories of Finn Mac Cumhaill, another hero similar in some ways to Cuchulainn. Of these, only one of the Mythological Cycle legends and some of the Cuchulainn stories are told here.

Welsh myths usually are referred to under the umbrella term *Mabinogion*. The *Mabinogion* is divided into four groupings known as "branches," each of which involves the adventures of a particular protagonist. The first branch is about Pwyll of Dyfed and is retold here. The other three branches tell the stories of Branwen daughter of Llyr, Manawydan son of Llyr, and Math son of Mathonwy, in that order. In addition to the four branches of the *Mabinogion*, there are a handful of so-called "native tales" that include the story of Culhwch and Olwen, which is also included in this collection.

Brittany is represented here by the tale of the drowned City of Ys from the *Barzazh Breiz*. This story has distinctly Celtic elements even if it never was an actual Celtic myth. Cornwall is represented by the story of Tristan and Iseult, a medieval Arthurian legend that has resonances with the ancient Irish tale "The Pursuit of Diarmuid and Grainne."

PART I

Ireland

The Children of Lir

This story is a perfect example of the ways Irish myth became filtered through a Christian lens in the Middle Ages. With very few exceptions, the characters of the story are all members of the Tuatha De Danann, who are a kind of echo of the old Celtic gods: they have magical powers, and if they are not quite immortal, they live hundreds of times longer than normal humans. In this story, the Children of Lir—whose name means "sea" and who apparently was some kind of Celtic ocean god—are turned into swans by their evil stepmother. In this form, they wander the world for more than nine hundred years, and their enchantment is only reversed after the Christianization of Ireland, when the rest of the Tuatha De have departed forever.

The Tuatha De Danann were a fair people, wise and learned in many arts. At a time, they met to elect who might be their king, and the two rivals for the throne were Lir and Bodb Derg, the son of the Dagda. The Tuatha De said that Bodb should be their king. This pleased Lir not at all, and he left the assembly without pledging fealty to Bodb Derg. The followers of the new king urged him to go after Lir, to assail his homestead, burn his house, and kill his people, but Bodb Derg refused, saying, "He will defend his home, and too many will die in the attempt. Besides, I am still king whether he gives me his fealty or not."

Now, Lir had a wife whom he loved very much. One day she fell ill. She was sick for three nights, and at the end of that time she died. Lir was stricken with grief, and he went about in mourning for a long time.

Word came to Bodb Derg of the loss of Lir. He took counsel with his nobles, and they all agreed that it would be well to try to help Lir. "For I have three foster daughters who are now of an age to marry," said Bodb, "and perhaps one of them would make a good wife for Lir."

And so messengers were sent to Lir, inviting him to the court of Bodb. The messengers said that if Lir were to offer fealty to Bodb, he might join his house to that of the Dagda by marrying one of the Bodb's foster daughters. Lir took thought on this and decided to accept. He gathered his nobles about him, and they went in fifty chariots to the court of Bodb Derg, where they were made very welcome.

At the feast, Bodb's foster daughters were seated on a bench with their foster mother, the wife of Bodb and queen of the Tuatha De. Bodb presented them to Lir, and their names were Aobh, Aoife, and Ailbhe. Bodb said to Lir, "You may choose which of my foster daughters you wish to have as your wife."

Lir replied, "I do not know which to choose, but I think it best to take the noblest of them, and this will be the eldest."

"Aobh is eldest," said Bodb, "and she shall be your wife this night if you desire it."

"It is my wish," said Lir, and so he and Aobh were wed that night.

And so Lir stayed at the court of Bodb Derg for a fortnight and then returned to his own home, where he made a great feast among his own people to celebrate his wedding to Aobh.

Soon enough, Aobh found herself with child, and when her time came she was delivered of twins. A daughter and a son she had, and they were named Fionnula and Aodh. Not long after that she became with child again and had two more children, boys named Fiachra and Conn, and in giving birth to them Aobh died. This caused Lir a grief so great that he might have died of it, had he not had four little ones to look after.

When the news of Aobh's death came to the court of Bodb Derg, everyone there went into mourning, for Aobh was a beautiful woman and much loved. Bodb Derg sorrowed for Lir, and once again took counsel with his nobles. They decided to invite him to court again and to give him Aobh's sister, Aoife, to be his wife. Messengers were sent to Lir with the offer from the king, and Lir said that he would gladly accept once his mourning was completed. When this was done, Lir went to the court of Bodb Derg, and there he took to wife Aoife.

Aoife and Lir lived together happily as man and wife for several years. Aoife never had any children of her own, but she doted on her stepchildren, and they loved her well. Indeed, everyone loved Aobh's children, for they were comely and a great delight. Their grandfather, the king, frequently visited Lir's household to be with them and also took them back to his court to stay from time to time, and all of Bodb Derg's court were entranced with them. And Lir especially loved his children and cared for them generously.

Aoife saw how the children captured the hearts of all who met them, and how well Lir loved them, and a worm of jealousy began to eat its way into her heart. Soon she had nothing but contempt for the children, which she took pains to hide by pretending to be ill. She lay ill for an entire year, all the while devising a wicked plan to be rid of them. And when the year was up, she announced that her illness had passed and that she wished to make a journey with the children. She called for a chariot to be harnessed, that she might take them to visit her foster father, the king.

Fionnula refused to get into the chariot saying, "I do not know where you mean to take us, but I know it is not to our grandfather's house. I had a dream last night, and I think you do not mean us well."

"My dear child," said Aoife, "how can that be? I wish nothing but the best for yourself and your brothers. We are going to visit Bodb Derg, as we often have done. Take no account of foolish dreams."

In the end, Fionnula could not resist Aoife and got into the chariot with her and her brothers. They drove on for a time, until they came to Loch Dairbhreach, the Lake of the Oaks. It was a fine summer's day, and very warm, so Aoife told the children to go into the lake and bathe to refresh themselves. The children removed their clothing, and when they had gone into the water Aoife struck them with her druid's wand, saying:

Luck be taken from you all

Children no more shall you be

In the shape of birds shall you go

And mourning cries fill the home of your father.

At this, the children were changed into four beautiful, white swans. But for all Aoife was able to change their shapes, she could not take from them the power of human speech. Fionnula reproached Aoife, saying, "Why have you done this to us? Surely we have never done any wrong to you deserving of such punishment. Know this, witch: we will seek help wherever it might be found, and soon enough you will have what you deserve for this deed. But until the day comes when you are held to account, at least have mercy enough to put bounds on our time under this enchantment."

Aoife was angered by Fionnuala's defiance, and said, "It were better had you not asked for that favor, for now I say to you that your own forms you will not find until the Lord of the North shall wed the Lady of the South, and until you have spent three hundred years on Loch Dairbhreach, and three hundred years on Sruth na Maoile between Ireland and Alba, and three hundred years between Irrus Domnann and Inis Gluaire."

But then Aoife looked upon the swan-children, her heart softened towards them in their plight, although she did not repent. She said, "Those shall be the bounds, but this I grant: that you shall always keep human speech, and that you shall always sing with the voices of the Sidhe, and the music of your song shall be the most beautiful in all the world and shall put mortal men to sweet sleep. And human thought also shall you keep, and the nobility of your spirits, that your hardship may be somewhat the less."

Then Aoife mounted her chariot and continued on to the court of Bodb Derg, leaving the swan-children lamenting behind her on the lake. When she reached her foster father's home, he asked her what had become of his grandchildren.

"I did not bring them," said Aoife, "for you no longer have the trust of Lir. He fears the love you bear for them and thinks that you will keep them here forever."

Bodb Derg was puzzled by this, for although the children were most dear to him he had never had any thought of taking them from their father, nor had he given Lir any cause to think that he might. Bodb therefore sent messengers to the home of Lir, on the pretext of asking after his children, saying that Aoife had told Bodb that Lir was keeping them back from him. By this did Lir understand the illness of Aoife, and that she had destroyed his children.

Lir called for horses to be saddled, and taking a band of picked men he set out the way Aoife had gone. When they came near the shores of Loch Dairbhreach, the swan-children heard the hoof beats and gathered on the shore near the road. They called out to the men with their own human voices, and Lir heard them. He and his companions halted, and Lir said to the swans, "Who are you, that you can speak and I can understand?"

"We are your own dear children," said Fionnula. "The wicked Aoife has enchanted us into the shape of swans."

Lir said, "How may I reverse this magic and give you back your own shapes?"

"There is no way that I know of," said Fionnula, "for she has put the enchantment on us for the space of nine-hundred years."

Then Lir and his companions cried out with grief, and they lamented there on the shores of the lake. When they were done with their weeping, Lir said, "Since you still have the power of speech and of human reason, will you not return home with us? For even in swan-shape you are still my own dear children, and I would have you with me."

"We may not leave Loch Dairbhreach," said Fionnula, "for that also is part of the enchantment. But rest you here tonight, and we shall sing for you a sweet song that will take from you your sorrows for a while."

And so this was done, that Lir and his companions made camp there for the night, and the children sang them to sleep with their sweet voices.

In the morning, Lir made ready to leave, but his heart was heavy that he could not take his children with him. He bade them a tearful farewell and then rode with his companions to the court of Bodb Derg. There Lir was given a fine welcome, but he gave no hint of what he had found at the lake until Bodb asked him where the children were, and Aoife was standing with him at the time.

"For that you shall have to ask your foster daughter, Aoife," said Lir, "for she has turned them into swans and bound them to the shores of Loch Dairbhreach."

At first Bodb would not believe Lir's tale, but finally he turned to Aoife and said, "Is this true?"

And she had to admit that it was. Bodb said to Aoife, "Which shape is the most abhorrent to you, were you put into it?"

Aoife said, "That of a demon of the air."

So Bodb took his own druid's wand and turned Aoife into a demon of the air. She flew three times around Bodb Derg's hall and then out an open window. She was never seen again in the shape of a woman, and for all anyone knows she flies about as a demon of the air still.

Then Bodb Derg summoned his retinue, and they went with Lir and his companions to live on the shore of Loch Dairbhreach where they might see the swan-children and listen to their song. After a time, more of the Tuatha De Danann came and made their homes there, as did the people of the Sons of Mil, for listening to the children's music was very sweet, and conversing with them was like speaking with human beings, but for them having the shape of swans. And so three hundred years passed at Loch Dairbhreach.

At the end of that three hundred years, Fionnula and her brothers went before their father and Bodb Derg and said, "Tomorrow we must fly away from here and go to Sruth na Maoile, for thus is the course of our enchantment."

Lir and Bodb Derg were greatly grieved by this and wept many tears, and the children sorrowed as well, for they did not wish to leave their father and grandfather behind. Finally they could tarry no longer. The swan-children spread their wings and took flight, and they did not stop until they arrived at Sruth na Maoile. And there the suffering of the children increased tenfold, for they were bound to stay on the waters of the cold, deep sea.

One evening as the sun was setting, Fionnula looked at the sky and saw that a storm was coming. She was afraid, for she could see that the storm was a strong one and likely she and her brothers would be lost to one another forever before it was over. She therefore said to them, "If the storm drives us apart, go when you can to Carraig na Ron, the Rock of the Seals. That is a place we all know, and we can meet there should the waves and wind divide us."

The boys agreed this was a wise plan. That night, the storm came upon them with waves as tall as houses and a rushing wind that howled and raged above the waters. As Fionnula had foreseen, she and her brothers were driven apart. When morning came, Fionnula struggled her way to Carraig na Ron, where she perched atop the rock and looked this way and that for sign of her brothers. Soon enough, they came to the rock themselves, all of them trembling and bedraggled from the ragings of the wind and sea. So Fionnula took Fiachra and Conn each under her wings, and Aodh under the feathers of her breast, and soon they were all dry and warm together.

And there they stayed, on the rock in the middle of the sea, until one night a deep frost came, with snow in it, and in the morning the swan-children found that the ice and frost had bound their feet to the rock and part of their wing feathers with them. With great effort they pried themselves loose, but the skin of their feet was left behind on the rock, as well as many of their feathers, and they were in great pain from their wounds. Slowly the swan-children made flight to shore, where they stayed during the day so that their hurts might be healed, but every night they returned to the waters of the strait, as they were bound by their stepmother's curse to do. And so a hundred years and more passed for them in this wise, in the daytime sometimes standing on Carraig na Ron, sometimes coming to the shores of Ireland or of Alba, but always spending the night on the tossing waves of the Sruth na Maoile.

One day the swan-children made their way to the mouth of the River Bann, and they saw coming towards them a company of horsemen. The men were warriors all, clad in bright cloaks with jeweled clasps and girt with swords, all of them astride horses as white as the swans' own feathers. The children waited until the horsemen were close enough, and then called out to them, for they thought that perhaps the riders were of the Tuatha De and so could give them news of their father and grandfather.

Upon hearing the voices of the swan-children, the men reined in their horses. Two of them dismounted and went over to where the swans were gathered.

"Greetings," they said. "Strange it is to hear swans speaking with our language, and we would know who you are."

"We are the Children of Lir," said Fionnula. "It is I, Fionnula, and my brothers Aodh and Fiachra and Conn, who were enchanted into the shape of swans by our stepmother, Aoife. Tell us now who you are, and who your people might be, for we hope you might have news for us of our father and grandfather."

"I am Aodh," said the first man, "and this is my brother, Fergus. We are the sons of Bodb Derg. We rejoice to have found you, for none has known what became of you after you left Loch Dairbhreach. We have sought for you for a long time."

"Glad we are as well," said Fionnula. "Tell us, if you will, how do our father and grandfather?"

"They are both well and residing in your father's house together," said Aodh Aithfhiosach, "and they are happy enough, save that they have wished sorely for news of you."

Then Fionnula and her brothers told Aodh and Fergus all they had suffered in their time on Sruth na Maoile, and it was grief indeed to the sons of Bodb Derg to hear this tale. They promised the swan-children to tell Lir and Bodb Derg their whole story, and to bring them their greetings. Lir and Bodb Derg rejoiced to hear that the children were yet living, although they had great sorrow for their sufferings, and again they wished heartily that there was something they could do to break the enchantment and bring the children home, but there was nothing to be done.

And so the rest of the three hundred years on Sruth na Maoile passed, until it came time for the swan-children to go to Irrus Domnann and Inis Gluaire. There they went in their swan-shapes, and there passed the next three hundred years, where they fared but a little better than they had on Sruth na Maoile.

At the end of that three hundred years, the swan-children were no longer bound to Irrus Domnann and Inis Gluaire, so they took flight for their father's home at Sidhe Fionnachaidh. All the way there the hearts of Fionnula and her brothers were glad and hopeful, for they heartily wished to see Lir again, and also Bodb Derg, and to be among their own people. But when they arrived, they knew not what to do, for Sidhe Fionnachaidh was abandoned and empty. The fields were overgrown with briars. The roofless house was abandoned to the wind and rain and the stones of the walls tumbling down into the turf. Fionnula and her brothers lamented together at the sight and sang a song so full of sorrow that had even the most hardened warrior heard it he would have died of a broken heart from the very pain of it. And so the swan-children passed that night in the ruins of their father's house, and in the morning returned to Inis Gluaire.

The swan-children stayed at times in Inis Gluaire, and at times flew to other places, but always they were in their swan-forms, and always they lamented the loss of their father and grandfather and of their people, the Tuatha De Danann. And in this wise they lived until after the coming of the Blessed St. Patrick to Ireland and St. Mochaomhog had built his church at Inis Gluaire.

One night, when they were at Inis Gluaire, they heard the ringing of a bell.

"What is that sound?" said Fiachra.

"That is the bell of Mochaomhog," said Fionnula. "Come, let us go and seek out that priest, for perhaps he has a way of ending our curse."

Mochaomhog's bell rang out until the end of Matins, and when it was done the swan-children began to sing the song of the Sidhe. Mochaomhog in his church heard their song and prayed to God that he might know whence it came. In a dream, he saw the swan-children gliding on the lake nearby, and so in the morning he went there to seek them. When he arrived at the lake, he saw the swan-children there, as they had been in his dream.

"Are you the Children of Lir?" said Mochaomhog, and the swan-children told him they were.

"Come with me," said the priest, "and be in my care, for it is given to me to see that all be made well for you."

The swan-children went with him then back to his church, and they lived with him. Every day, Mochaomhog said Holy Mass, which the swan-children reverently attended. Mochaomhog also had silver collars fashioned for them, with a chain between each pair of collars. Fionnula was linked with Aodh, her twin, and Fiachra and Conn were linked likewise. The swan-children lived in peace and great contentment with Mochaomhog, and he cared for them well.

Now, at that time there was a king in Connacht, and his name was Lairgnen and his wife was named Deoch. And their marriage was the fulfillment of Aoife's condition that the Lord of the North be wed to the Lady of the South. Word that the Children of Lir were living at Mochaomhog's church came to the ears of Deoch, and she wished to have them brought to her. Lairgnen then sent messengers to Mochaomhog, asking him to send the birds to the queen, but the priest refused. This angered the king greatly, so he went to Inis Gluaire himself to take the birds from Mochaomhog, by force if need be.

But when Lairgnen demanded the swans, Mochaomhog said, "I shall not give them to you, though you be king of all the world."

At that the king rose up in anger and went to where the swan-children were hiding in the church. Lairgnen took them in his hands, thinking to carry them home to his wife, but as soon as he touched them their swan-forms fell away. Lairgnen found himself grasping the arms of a woman and three men, all white-haired and withered with great age. This frightened Lairgnen so greatly that he ran out of the church and straight back to his home without once looking back.

Then Fionnula called out to Mochaomhog, "Come to us, quickly, for our death is upon us. Listen to my last request, and do what I ask for love of myself and my brothers. Bury us all together, with Conn at my left and Fiachra at my right, and my brother Aodh in my arms. And do you now baptize all of us in the name of your God that we might be with him in paradise."

And so all this was done. Mochaomhog baptized the four that very day. They passed soon afterwards, and were buried together in the manner Fionnula asked, with stone placed above them having their names carved into it in ogham. Mochaomhog and the people of his parish mourned the death of the swan-children, whose souls were taken into paradise after their long lives of suffering.

And that is all that is known of the Children of Lir.

The Birth of Cuchulainn

As befits a Celtic hero, Cuchulainn is born not once but three times, a mystical number that denotes Otherworldly origins. His first birth is of Otherworldly parents, his second of the god Lug, and his third of a human father. We know that the first family is of the Otherworld first because of the flock of birds that lead Conchobor and Deichtine to them, and also by the birthplace at Brugh na Boinne, home to an important series of ancient pagan tombs that were considered to be passages to the Otherworld.

Tales such as these often contain hints about ancient Irish culture, such as the practice of noble families sending their children out to

15

foster. Taking in the child of another noble family was seen as both a right and a privilege and could confer status on the foster family.

The people of Ulster once were beset by a large flock of birds. The birds came to the plain of Emain, and wherever they came to rest on the ground they ate whatever grew there. The crops were being ruined, and the people of Ulster were angry and afraid.

Conchobor went with his nobles in nine chariots to chase after the flock and make them go away if they could. Deichtine, the sister of Conchobor, went with them, driving the chariot for her brother. Conall and Laegire and Bricriu, the finest of the warriors of Ulster, accompanied Conchobor and Deichtine as well.

Conchobor and his company chased the birds across Sliab Fuait. They chased them across Edmonn and Breg Plain. Nine score birds there were, flying always before them, singing a graceful song. As the chariots drew closer, the warriors could see that the birds wore silver collars, and that pairs of the birds were linked together with chains of silver. The day wore on, and Conchobor and his company could come no closer to them. As the sun set, they watched three of the birds separate from the flock and fly away.

The men of Ulster chased the birds as far as Brugh na Boinne, but then night fell and they had to stop. Conchobor told his company to loose the horses from their traces, and to look for someplace they might shelter for the night. While the others looked after the horses, Conall and Bricriu went to find shelter. They found a house standing by itself in a lonely place. In the house was a man and his wife, and the wife was with child. They told Conall and Bricriu that their company would be made most welcome.

Conall and Bricriu returned and told Conchobor what they had found, and soon the whole company was lodged in the tiny house that stood alone on the plain. There was food and drink in plenty, and the Ulstermen enjoyed themselves well. While they were at table, the man came to Conchobor and said, "Please help us. My wife is in her pains."

Deichtine left the company and went to help the woman. Soon the woman was delivered of a fine baby boy. There was also a mare at the house, who gave birth to two foals. This happened exactly when the woman gave birth to her son. Deichtine nursed the boy, and the warriors gave him the foals as a gift.

When all this was done, the company lay down to sleep. But when morning came, they awoke to find that the house had vanished, along with the man and the woman and the mare. In the folds of Conchobor's cloak lay the baby, and with their own horses stood the two foals. The men looked about and found that the flock of birds also had vanished. At that, they harnessed their horses and returned to Emain, where Deichtine tended the baby as though he were her own. The baby grew well under Deichtine's care, but one day he took sick and died, and Deichtine's grief was very great.

One time after this, Deichtine became thirsty. She took a drink of water but did not notice that a small creature was in the cup. She swallowed the creature along with the water. That night, Deichtine had a dream. In the dream, a man came to her. He was handsome and well-built, obviously a mighty warrior. The man said to her, "I it was who brought you and your company to Brugh na Boinne. My son it was that you cared for as your own. My name is Lug mac Ethnenn. I give you another son this night, and you shall name him Setanta. You shall raise him with the foals who were also born at Brugh na Boinne."

Soon afterwards, Deichtine found herself with child. But she was not wed, so the people of Ulster whispered among themselves that maybe Conchobor had lain with his own sister one night, when he was drunk. This brought shame on Conchobor, so he wed her to Sualdam mac Roich.

On her wedding night, Deichtine did not want to lie with her husband while she was with child. She fell ill, and she vomited.

When she vomited, the creature she had swallowed came out of her body. Having thus purified herself, she went to her new husband and lay with him. She was made with child by him, and when her time came, she bore a son. She named the boy Setanta.

When Deichtine's son was born, the nobles of Conchobor's court argued about who was to take him in to foster. Each of them boasted about his wealth and skills, and about how he would be the best choice to raise the boy. Then Conchobor said, "Let us not argue in this fashion. My sister Finnchaem will care for the boy until we return to Emain, and there we will ask judgement of Morann, who is wise and judges fairly."

It was done as Conchobor said. They all returned to Emain, and Finnchaem cared for Setanta. They went to Morann and told him the issue that needed to be decided. Morann said, "Conchobor should be his foster father because he is Setanta's kinsman. The rest of you also shall foster him and teach him the things you know. This boy will be a hero and the defender of Ulster, and all of you shall help him reach his destiny."

The men of Ulster thought this a very fair judgement, so Setanta was given first to Finnchaem and Amergin in their house at Imrith Fort on the Plain of Murtheimne until such time as he was old enough to learn what the others had to teach.

How Cuchulainn Got His Name

Like many heroes, Cuchulainn—whose boyhood name was Setanta, as we have seen—is possessed of prodigious strength and skill from an early age. In this story, we learn how he got the name Cuchulainn, which means "Hound of Culann." The translation of the Irish word cu *as "hound" is important because it refers to a particular kind of dog, a noble animal and a hunter—or, as in this tale, a fierce watchdog—while the word* gadhar *refers to a more ordinary dog.*

Hurling, which is played by Cuchulainn and Conchobor's boy-troop, is an ancient Irish sport that is still played today. Players use "hurleys," which are something like hockey sticks with rounded heads, to hit or carry a small ball. Hands and feet also can be used to move the ball. Points are scored by hitting the ball over the opponent's goalposts or into a net that is guarded by the opponent's goalkeeper.

Fidchell, *the game played by Conchobor in this tale, is likewise very ancient. Sometimes the word* fidchell *is translated as "chess," but while we know that* fidchell *was some kind of board game played by two opponents having an equal number of pieces, no boards, pieces, or rules for* fidchell *have survived, so it is unclear exactly how closely it might have matched the game of chess as we know it today.*

Thrice-born Setanta grew to boyhood in a great house on the plain of Muirthemne. One day, when Setanta was five years old, tales of the boy-troop of Emain Macha came to his ears. He heard that King Conchobor liked to divide his day into three parts: one part was for watching the boy-troop at their games, of which hurling was chiefest; one was for playing *fidchell*; and the third was for eating and drinking and listening to the music of minstrels until he felt sleepy and retired to his chamber.

Setanta went to his mother and said, "Mother, I should like to go to Emain Macha. I should like to meet the boy-troop of Conchobor and see whether I can best them at their sports."

"Oh, Setanta," said his mother, "you should not go. You are too young, and there is no warrior to go with you to ensure your safety."

"I do not need a warrior to protect me," said Setanta. "And I will not wait. I mean to go now, if you would but tell me the way."

Setanta's mother reluctantly agreed, and so told him how to get to Emain Macha. The next day, Setanta set out for the court of

Conchobor. He took with him his shield, his brass hurley, his silver ball, his javelin, and his toy spear, and with these things he amused himself on his long journey. First he used the hurley to hit the ball, driving it a long distance in front of him. Then he threw the hurley the same distance in the same direction, and then the javelin likewise, and then the spear. This done, he would run after all of these and pick up the ball, the hurley, and the javelin, and then catch the spear before it hit the ground.

Soon enough, Setanta arrived at Emain Macha. There he found Conchobor's boy-troop at their sport. Three times fifty boys there were, all playing on a green field. Some were playing hurley, while others were learning warrior's craft with Conchobor's son, Follamain. Without speaking a word to any of them, Setanta dove into the hurley game. He caught the ball between his knees and held it there, and none of the boys could touch it. Holding the ball this way, he went down the field and then put the ball over the post for a goal. The boy-troop watched this in amazement.

Follamain saw it also and cried out, "Who is this upstart who enters your game without first getting your guarantee of protection, as is your custom? All of you now, fall upon him and kill him, for he has no right to be here."

The boy-troop immediately took their hurleys and threw them at Setanta's head, but he parried each and every one of them with his own hurley. Then the boys pelted Setanta with balls, but he kept these off with his hands and arms. When the boys flung their little spears at him, Setanta caught every spear with his shield, and so was unharmed. Then Setanta waded in among the boys and laid low fifty of them, and they the best and strongest and most skilled of the whole troop.

As Conchobor sat playing *fidchell* with Fergus, five of the boys went speeding past, trying to escape Setanta's wrath, and Setanta himself close on their heels. Conchobor called out to Setanta.

"Stop, there!" he said. "What game is this that you play with my boy-troop? Why do you use them so ill?"

"That question you might ask of them as well," said Setanta, "for here I am come from a distant land, and no guest's welcome to meet me."

"I see," said Conchobor. "Who are you, and who are your parents?"

"I am Setanta, son of Sualdam and your sister, Deichtine, and I did not expect to be treated as an enemy here."

"Did you not know that it is the custom of my boy-troop that all outsiders must beg their protection before joining them at their sport?" said Conchobor.

"I did not," said Setanta, "otherwise this I would have done from the first."

Conchobor therefore went to the boy-troop and said, "You shall now pledge to this lad your protection," and the troop agreed that they would do so.

Then Conchobor said to Setanta, "What are you going to do now?"

"I shall offer the boy-troop my protection."

"Promise it to me, then," said Conchobor. "Swear it now."

"I do swear," said Setanta.

Then the boys returned to their play, and those that Setanta had knocked down were helped up and given care for their hurts.

One day, when Setanta was six years old, Conchobor set out with some of his choicest warriors and Cathbad the druid to attend a feast at the home of Culann the Smith. According to his custom, Conchobor first went to the playing-field to see what the boys were doing and ask their blessing upon his journey. When he arrived, he watched the boys playing one game after another, the entire troop against Setanta, and in each game Setanta defeated the lot of them with ease. Conchobor was amazed by this, and invited Setanta to go to the feast with him.

"I thank you," said Setanta, "but first I must finish my sport with the boy-troop. I will meet you there later."

Conchobor went ahead to the feast with his warriors. When they arrived, Culann greeted them well and said, "Is this all the company? I ask this because I have a great hound that guards my livestock. He is cunning and vicious, and so strong that it takes three men holding his three chains to keep him back when he is roused. I am going to let him go after the gate is closed and you and your company are inside."

"There are no others following after," said Conchobor, for he had forgotten that Setanta would be joining them when he was done with his play.

The company sat down to the feast Culann had made, and they were enjoying themselves well when they heard the baying of the hound outside. Then Conchobor blanched, for he remembered that Setanta was to follow them, and the hound was loose in the field. Conchobor ran to the window at the sound of the hound's baying, as did Culann and the rest of the company. With great dismay they watched little Setanta making his way across the field, amusing himself with his hurley and ball by striking the ball and then running to catch it before it hit the ground, and the great hound racing towards him with such speed that not even the fastest chariot could have caught him before he reached the lad.

The hound made for Setanta, its maw wide open to swallow him at one gulp. But Setanta did not even flinch. Instead, he took his hurley and struck the ball mightily at the hound. He hit the ball with such force that it went straight down the hound's gullet and passed all the way through its body without stopping. Then Setanta grabbed the hound by its hind legs and dashed its back against a tree so hard that its limbs were forced right out of their sockets.

Culann, Conchobor, and the warriors came running out to see what had become of Setanta, and found the boy standing there next to the remains of the hound. Culann lamented when he saw that the hound was dead. "O that I had never given this feast!" he said. "That hound was the best that ever was, and like part of my family. He guarded my household and my property, and never shall his like be seen again!"

"Do not grieve," said Setanta, "for I myself will rear a pup to take his place, and he will do the same duty and more for you. And until that pup is ready, I myself will be your hound, guarding your household and your property, and all Murtheimne Plain besides."

Culann accepted this as payment of Setanta's debt, and Conchobor also said that it was a fair offer. Then Cathbad the druid said, "Your name from henceforth shall be Cuchulainn, the Hound of Culann."

Setanta pronounced himself well pleased with this, and he used that name to the end of his days.

PART II
Wales

Pwyll, Prince of Dyfed

This story, from the first branch of the Welsh Mabinogion, *has many hallmarks of Celtic myth, especially in the fluid boundaries between the human world and the Otherworld. The first indication that the human Pwyll has stepped over that boundary is the color of the strange hunting pack: the hounds are white with red ears, a clear sign that they belong to an Otherworldly huntsman. The second half of the story also partakes of ancient Celtic ideas about the Otherworld: a perch on a perilous hill that allows one to see things that might not otherwise be seen; a mysterious horse and rider who cannot be chased down; and a miraculous child who shows precocious growth and prodigious strength.*

Readers of Lloyd Alexander's Chronicles of Prydain *will recognize this story as the source of the names Arawn and Annuvin (spelled Annwfn in the Welsh original). In Alexander's telling, Arawn is an evil dark lord and Annuvin his fearsome realm. In this tale, however, Arawn is not drawn as a villain, and while the Annwfn of the* Mabinogion *definitely is in the Otherworld, it is not a dark or forbidding place at all. Alexander likewise altered the characters of Pwyll and Pryderi to suit his own stories which, although drawing on the* Mabinogion, *are not retellings of those ancient tales.*

Once there was a Prince of Dyfed, and his name was Pwyll. Pwyll liked nothing better than to go hunting, and so one morning he and his companions mounted their horses and took their hounds out into the countryside, where they hoped to catch a fine stag. They had not been hunting long when Pwyll and his hounds became separated from his friends. As Pwyll looked about trying to find where the others had gone, he heard the cry of hounds, but it was not the cry of his own pack. Pwyll rode into a clearing, where he saw the other pack of hounds chasing a stag.

Pwyll had never seen hounds like these before. Their coats were white as snow, but their ears were red as blood. Before Pwyll could call his own hounds to him, the other pack attacked the stag and brought it down. Pwyll chased away the strange dogs and allowed his own pack to eat of the carcass.

While Pwyll's dogs were eating, a man rode up on a dapple-grey horse. He carried a hunting horn on a fine chain, and his clothes were all of a soft grey color. The rider said, "Sir, I recognize you, but I will not greet you."

Pwyll said, "Perhaps you are of a rank that does not require you to greet me."

"No," said the rider, "it is not rank that prevents me, but your own grave discourtesy."

"What discourtesy have I done?" said Pwyll.

"Why, nothing more than chasing away the pack that brought down the stag, only to feed your own hounds upon it," said the rider. "However, I do not mean to take revenge on you for it. Rather I will sound your shame throughout the whole land, even to the value of one hundred stags."

Pwyll said, "If I have done discourtesy to you, then I shall make it right. This I shall do according to your station, but first I must know your name and where is your country."

"In my country, I am a king," said the rider.

"My lord, I greet you and wish you good day," said Pwyll. "What is the name of your country?"

"I come from Annwfn," said the rider, "and my name is Arawn, king of Annwfn."

"My lord," said Pwyll, "how shall I make it right between us?"

"I shall tell you," said the rider. "There is another king in Annwfn, and his name is Hafgan. He continually fights with me. I wish him to harry me no more. If you want to earn my friendship, you must rid me of him."

"That I will gladly do," said Pwyll, "if you tell me how to go about it."

Arawn said, "You will come to my palace in Annwfn, and for the space of a year you shall wear my face and form so that none of my courtiers will be able to tell the difference between us. You shall share a bed with my own wife, and neither shall she know that you are not me. This you shall do for the space of one year, and at the end of that time we will meet again in this place."

"I do not understand how this will put an end to your enemy," said Pwyll. "Also I do not know this Hafgan; how will I find him so that I may rid you of him?"

"I have an agreement to meet him at the ford a year from tonight. If you go there in my place, in my shape, you shall give him one blow. He will die of it. But you must not give him more than one, no matter how much he asks you to do so. Because every other time I have faced him, it did not matter how many times I struck him, he was always as strong as before."

"I shall do as you ask," said Pwyll, "but what will become of my own lands while I am gone?"

"I shall assume your form in the same way you shall assume mine, and none in your lands will know the difference," said Arawn.

"I accept these terms gladly," said Pwyll. "You have but to show me the way to your court."

Arawn then told him the way to his palace. He told Pwyll to go straight to the court, and to behave as though he belonged there, for none of the people would be able to tell he was not Arawn.

When Pwyll arrived, he saw that Arawn's court was indeed a fine place. The palace was made of well-hewn stone, and the halls and chambers were lined with tapestries and carved wood. Pwyll was greeted warmly by many servants, who helped him change his clothes to ready him for the banquet. Then Pwyll went into the hall, and marveled at the many warriors gathered there, each one of them obviously a champion.

Pwyll took his seat at table, with the queen on his right and a man he supposed was an earl on his left. The queen was the most beautiful woman he had ever seen, and after but a little speech with her Pwyll saw that she was the most gracious as well. The evening passed with much enjoyment, and soon it was time for bed. The queen and Pwyll went up to their chamber together, and when they climbed into bed Pwyll turned his back to her and said not another word until the morning, and in this wise they slept together for the space of a year.

For the whole of that year, Pwyll spent his time happily in hunting and feasting with his new companions, until it came time for him to go to the ford for the meeting he had promised to attend. He went to the ford accompanied by a band of his noblemen. They arrived to find Hafgan there before them, with his own retinue of picked warriors, and just as it was at the court of Annwfn, none could tell that Pwyll was not Arawn.

One of Arawn's noblemen came forward and said, "This is a dispute between kings, over lands and domains. The dispute is between them and them alone. No one is to interfere in their fight."

Then Hafgan and Pwyll took up their swords and shields. They mounted their chargers and advanced into the ford. At the very first clash of arms, Pwyll clove Hafgan's shield in two with a blow so mighty it shattered Hafgan's armor and sent him reeling back over his horse's crupper and into the river, and Hafgan knew that he had received his death-blow.

Hafgan got to his knees and said, "My lord, by what right do you deal me a death-blow? I claimed nothing from you: you started this dispute to take lands from me. I do not know why you think I must die here in the ford, but since you have started down that path you may as well finish it. Kill me now!"

"My lord," said Pwyll, "I may yet regret what I have done to you. But I will not kill you. You must find someone else to do that deed."

Hafgan turned to his nobles and said, "Take me away from here. I soon shall die. I will not be your king any longer."

Pwyll said to Hafgan's nobles, "I give you time to take counsel to see which of you must now owe fealty to me."

Hafgan's nobles replied that all of them now were vassals of Arawn, and that Arawn was now the sole king in Annwfn. Pwyll then received their fealty and set about the work of ordering the realm of Annwfn.

After this was done, Pwyll set out for the place where he was to meet Arawn, and he found Arawn there before him. The two men greeted each other well.

Arawn said, "May God bless you well for all you have done, for I have heard all about it."

Then Arawn returned himself to his own form, and did the same for Pwyll. Then the two men bade farewell to one another and went to their own homes.

When Arawn arrived back at his own court, he greeted everyone very warmly, for he had missed them while he was away. Everyone remarked on how friendly Arawn was being, for they did not know that he had been elsewhere. That night there was a great banquet, and when it came time to go to bed Arawn was very affectionate with his wife, and he made joyful love to her. She wondered what had happened to change his mood so much, since he had not touched her for an entire year.

She thought long about this. When Arawn woke up, he spoke to her, but she did not answer. He did this many times, but each time his wife remained silent.

"Wife," said Arawn, "why will you not speak to me?"

"It is because for a full year you have said not one word to me when we have been in this bed."

"But we have always talked together here," said Arawn.

"Husband, I tell you that for the space of a whole year you have said not one word to me when we have been together in bed, neither have you touched me nor so much as looked at me."

Arawn thought how steadfast and faithful Pwyll had been to him, and was grateful. Then he turned to his wife and said, "My lady, I do not blame you for your anger. But I must tell you that for the space of that year it was not I who shared this bed with you." And then he told her the whole story, and she also marveled at how faithful Pwyll had been.

Now, as Arawn was enjoying his homecoming, Pwyll also returned to his own realm. He asked his nobles how well they thought he had ruled them for the past year, and to a man they agreed they had never seen the realm so well ordered. Then Pwyll told them the whole story, saying that they owed thanks to Arawn for his diligence. The nobles agreed that Arawn had proved a stout friend to Pwyll. But then they said, "Surely you will continue to rule in the same wise as Arawn had done?" And Pwyll swore that he would do so.

Pwyll and Arawn continued to be friends. They paid visits to each other's courts and went hunting together, and from time to time would exchange gifts of hounds or horses or weapons, or of other things they found that they thought might make a fine present for the other to enjoy. And because Pwyll had ruled so faithfully in Arawn's stead, he was no longer styled Prince of Dyfed, but rather Pwyll Pen Annwfn.

There came a time when Pwyll went to visit his court at Arberth. The court held a great banquet in his honor, and after he had eaten and drunk Pwyll went to stretch his legs. He headed for a mound that was situated near the court, and this place was called Gorsedd Arberth. One of his nobles saw which way he was going and said, "My lord, I do not counsel you to walk upon that mound, for it is said that if a nobleman ascends it he will not come down again save he has been wounded or else seen some marvel."

"I do not fear being wounded," said Pwyll, "for surely I am safe here among a retinue of so many champions, and the sight of a marvel would be most welcome."

Pwyll ascended the mound, and some of his noblemen came with him. When they got to the top, they sat down. Soon enough, they saw a maiden approaching. She was dressed in the finest silk embroidered with golden thread, and she was riding a milk-white horse.

"Does anyone recognize that woman?" said Pwyll.

The nobles all said that they did not know her.

"Someone must go and find out who she is," said Pwyll.

One of the nobles ran down the hill, but the woman had already ridden past, and no matter how fast the man ran, he could not catch up with her. The noble returned to Pwyll and said, "My lord, no one will be able to catch her on foot."

"Go and get the fastest horse in the stable," said Pwyll. "Follow her, and find out who she is."

The nobleman did as Pwyll bid him. He took the fastest horse in the stable and galloped after the woman. The woman's horse seemed to be going at an easy pace, but no matter how fast the nobleman rode, he could come no closer to her than when he first espied her on the road. Soon his horse tired, and he had to turn back. He went to Pwyll and told him what had happened.

"I see," said Pwyll. "There is something magical afoot here. We can do no more for now."

Then he and his nobles returned to the court, where they spent the rest of their day.

The next day there was another banquet. Pwyll again set out for the mound after he had eaten and drunk, but this time he took a fast horse with him, and a servant to ride it. They had barely reached the top of the mound when they saw the lady on the white horse approaching on the highway, just as had happened the previous day.

Pwyll told the servant, "Quick! Mount, and go after her. Find out who she is and where she lives."

By the time the lad was mounted and on the highway, the lady had already passed. The servant spurred his horse to catch up with her, but no matter how fast he galloped he could not draw any closer, even though the lady's mount seemed to be going at an easy pace. The servant tried slowing his horse, to see whether he might be able to catch her if he matched her pace, but neither was this of any use. He tried once more to ride hard after her, but he could not catch her, and she never varied her speed. The servant returned to the court and told Pwyll what had happened. Pwyll realized that it was of no use to try to chase her, although he was convinced that she had a message to deliver if only someone were able to speak with her.

That evening and the next day passed in the same fashion as the ones before, and at the end of the day's feast Pwyll returned to the mound with a company of his nobles. But this time he brought his own horse and wore his own spurs. Soon enough, they saw the lady approaching on her horse. Pwyll mounted as she rode past. He galloped after her, thinking that surely he would be able to catch her, for no horse in the land could match his own for fire and speed. But it was no different for him than for any of the others who had tried: however hard he rode she always stayed the same distance away, going at the same easy pace.

Finally Pwyll called out, "My lady! For the sake of your own beloved, I beg that you wait for me."

"That I will do gladly," said the woman, "but your horse might have preferred it if you had asked me earlier."

The lady waited for Pwyll, and as he drew near she pulled away the veil that had been covering her face.

"My lady," said Pwyll, "where are you from, and where is it that you are going?"

"I go where I will, on business of my own," she said. "And I am very glad to speak with you."

"I am grateful also that you will speak with me," said Pwyll, and he saw that she was more beautiful than any woman he had ever seen before.

"My lady," said Pwyll, "may I know what business you are on?"

"Certainly," she replied. "My business is to speak with you."

"Surely that is the best business you could undertake," said Pwyll. "If it please you, may I know your name?"

"I am Rhiannon, daughter of Hyfaidd Hen. My father wishes me to marry a man of his choosing. But I do not wish that marriage, because of the love I bear for you. I will not marry another, unless you say you do not want me. But that is why I have ridden by the mound these past days: to have your answer whether we shall wed or not."

Pwyll said, "I swear solemnly that if I were given all the women in the world to choose from, I would choose only you to be my bride."

"I am well pleased," said Rhiannon. "You must arrange to meet with me, then, before I am wed to another."

"I shall meet with you at the time and place that you choose," said Pwyll.

"Very well," said Rhiannon. "Meet me at the court of Hyfaidd, a year from tonight. I shall have a feast prepared for you when you come."

Pwyll agreed to Rhiannon's plan. Then they took their leave of each other, and Pwyll returned to the mound where he found his nobles still waiting for him. They asked him many times what had happened while he was away, but he would not answer.

When the time came for his meeting with Rhiannon, Pwyll called to himself a retinue of ninety-nine nobles. They went to the court of Hyfaidd where they were made most welcome. At the banquet, Pwyll sat with Hyfaidd to one side of him and Rhiannon to the other, and the rest of the company sat according to their stations. They ate and drank and enjoyed themselves greatly, and while they were enjoying themselves a tall youth with auburn hair strode into the hall. He walked up to Pwyll and greeted him well.

"You are most welcome, friend," said Pwyll. "Come, take a seat, and meat and drink will be brought to you."

"I thank you, but I shall not sit," said the youth. "For I have come to ask of you a favor."

"You have my leave to ask," said Pwyll, "and whatever I may do for you, I shall do or see done."

Rhiannon turned to Pwyll in alarm. "You should not have given your word so freely!" she said.

"It is too late, my Lady," said the youth, "for his word is now given, and in the presence of witnesses."

"Make your request," said Pwyll.

"You are here tonight to wed the woman I love most," said the youth, "and I therefore ask that she become my bride, and that this feast before you tonight become my wedding feast."

At this Pwyll said nothing.

"Holding your peace avails you nothing," said Rhiannon. "Never was any man more foolhardy than you have been tonight, for this is the man my father wanted me to marry against my will."

"My lady, I beg your pardon," said Pwyll, "for I did not know who he was."

"He is Gwawl son of Clud, a nobleman with a large retinue. And now you must give me over to him, for you have pledged your word to do so."

"My lady, I could never give you to another man," said Pwyll.

"You must. But never fear: he shall never have me if you do as I say," said Rhiannon.

"What must I do?" said Pwyll.

Then Rhiannon whispered to Pwyll her plan how she would set herself free from Gwawl. Rhiannon gave Pwyll a small bag and told him that he should come to the feast she would make for Gwawl in a year's time, but that Pwyll should disguise himself as a beggar. He should ask Gwawl to fill the bag with food and that he would leave when the bag was full. Except the bag was magical: no matter how much food was put into the bag, it would only ever be half full unless a man of the very highest quality climbed inside and stamped down the food. Surely Gwawl would want to prove his quality and would climb inside the bag. Then Pwyll could close the bag up tight with Gwawl inside it, and he would be in Pwyll's power. Once Gwawl was Pwyll's prisoner, Pwyll could summon his warriors to invade the court and subdue Gwawl's retinue.

While Rhiannon was speaking to Pwyll, Gwawl became impatient. "My lord, you have given your word, and I wait for you to make good upon it."

Pwyll said, "I will grant your request insofar as I have power to grant it."

Then Rhiannon said to Gwawl, "Me you shall have, but the feast is not Pwyll's to give. I have already given it to him and to his retinue. Come back a year from tonight, and I shall prepare a feast for you, and we shall be wed at that time."

Gwawl agreed to these terms, and departed from the court of Hyfaidd.

At the appointed time, Rhiannon made ready a feast for Gwawl and his retinue. Pwyll also made ready. He disguised himself in ragged, dirty clothes and wore boots with holes in them. He took with him his own retinue of ninety-nine warriors, all armed and ready for battle. The warriors he hid in the forest outside the court of Hyfaidd, while he himself limped up to the gate. Pretending to be a beggar, Pwyll went to the gate of the court and was allowed in, for it was the custom there that no beggar be turned away. Pwyll went into the hall where Gwawl sat with Rhiannon on his right hand, and Hyfaidd on his left.

Gwawl saw the beggar approaching and said, "Welcome to you. What is it that you want?"

"I come to beg for food, my lord," said Pwyll, "food to fill my small bag, here."

Gwawl ordered his servants to give food to the beggar, thinking that such a small bag would be quickly filled and he would be rid of this pest. But no matter how many loaves of bread or haunches of meat the servants put into the bag, it was never full.

"What is taking so long?" said Gwawl. "Why is that bag not yet full?"

"My lord," said Pwyll, "it will only be full if a nobleman of the highest quality should step in and stamp down what is already inside."

Rhiannon said to Gwawl, "You are such a nobleman. No one else here could do that deed, I am sure of it!"

Wishing to prove himself to Rhiannon and to the court, Gwawl said, "I will gladly do this thing."

Gwawl then climbed into the bag. Quickly Pwyll shook the bag and turned it about so that Gwawl would be head over heels. Then Pwyll pulled the drawstrings tight and tied them so that Gwawl could not escape. Pwyll threw off his rags and took out his hunting horn, which he had concealed in his beggar's clothes, and blew upon it a mighty blast. The warriors he had hidden in the trees came rushing into the court at Pwyll's signal. They subdued Gwawl's retinue and took them prisoner. Once that was done, each of Pwyll's warriors went up to the bag and struck it a blow, saying "What is in here?"

From inside the bag Gwawl said, "My lord, surely it is not fitting for you to kill me this way, while I am tied up inside a bag and cannot defend myself."

Hyfaidd Hen said, "Surely what he says is true. He is a nobleman, and this is not fitting."

"Yes, I agree," said Pwyll. "So what is to be done with him?"

"I know what should be done, if you will hear me," said Rhiannon to Pwyll. "You now have the power in this court. It is for you now to grant favors here. Have Gwawl make presents to all who are now here, and make him promise that he will seek neither claim nor vengeance against you for what has happened here this day."

"I accept those terms gladly," said Gwawl, still inside the bag.

"That is good advice, and I also accept," said Pwyll, "if guarantors may be found for Gwawl."

"I will stand surety for him," said Hyfaidd, "until his nobles can do that for him."

At that, Gwawl was let out of the bag. When the nobles who would stand surety for Gwawl had also been set free, and when they had agreed to act on Gwawl's behalf as needed, Gwawl was given permission to withdraw so that he could bathe and have his wounds dressed before he departed for his own lands.

Then Hyfaidd's hall was prepared once again for a feast, this time to celebrate the wedding of Rhiannon and Pwyll, and when the feast was done Rhiannon and Pwyll went to their chamber, and there they delighted in one another and became man and wife. The next day, Pwyll and Rhiannon arose early. Pwyll went to the court, where he heard the pleas of suppliants and musicians. He gave them all they asked, and no one went away unsatisfied.

When this was done, Pwyll went to Hyfaidd and said, "I wish to set out for Dyfed tomorrow, with your blessing."

Hyfaidd said, "This is well. Tell me when Rhiannon is to follow you."

"My lord," said Pwyll, "I wish that she should come with me when I go."

Hyfaidd agreed to this, and in the morning Pwyll and Rhiannon went to Dyfed. They stopped at Pwyll's court at Arberth, where they found a feast awaiting them. All the nobles of Dyfed were gathered there, to celebrate the marriage of Pwyll and Rhiannon. To each and every one Rhiannon gave some precious gift, according to their station. For three years after that, the nobles were content with the rule of Pwyll and his bride, but at the end of that time they became restless, for Pwyll did not yet have an heir.

The nobles came before Pwyll and said, "My lord, we counsel that you take another wife, that you may have a son. You cannot continue to rule us if you cannot produce an heir."

Pwyll replied, "I hear your words. I beg you give us another year, and if at the end of that time I have no heir, I will do as you ask."

The nobles agreed to Pwyll's request. Before the end of the year, Rhiannon found herself with child. When her time came, she was delivered of a fine baby boy. Women were set to watch over mother and child after the birth, but one by one the women fell asleep, as did Rhiannon herself. When the women awoke, they found that the baby was missing.

"What shall we do?" said one woman. "Surely we will all be put to death for this."

The others agreed that this was likely.

Then another woman said, "I know what we should do. In the mews there is a hound who has had a litter of pups. Take some of the pups, and kill them. Smear the blood all over the queen's face and hands, and put the bones in the bed with her. We all will then swear that she killed the child herself."

The women agreed that this was a good plan, and it was done. When Rhiannon awoke, she asked where her child had gone.

"Do not ask us, my lady," said the women. "You have only to look about you to see what became of him. And you have only to look at the bruises upon our arms to see how we had to fight you, and still you were able to destroy your son."

Rhiannon looked upon the women and said, "You must not tell lies about me. I cannot protect you if you do not tell me the truth."

The women swore that they were truthful. Rhiannon urged them again and again not to tell lies, but the women swore each time that they were telling the truth.

Soon enough word of the women's story came to the ears of Pwyll and his nobles. The nobles insisted that Pwyll divorce Rhiannon and take another wife. But Pwyll refused, saying, "I need divorce my wife only if she is barren, and that she is not. I have an heir. But if my wife has done wrong, then she should be punished."

Rhiannon took counsel with her advisers, and soon it was decided that it was best for her to accept whatever punishment she should be given. And this was her punishment: that for the space of seven years she should sit outside the gate of the court at Arberth and tell her story to whoever asked, and that she should then offer to carry them to the court on her back. Very few asked her to carry them. And in this wise Rhiannon passed part of a year.

It was at this time that the lord of Gwent Is Coed was a man named Teyrnon Twrf Liant. Teyrnon owned the finest mare in all the land, and every foal she produced was the best to be found anywhere. She would always foal on May Eve, but by morning the foal disappeared. Teyrnon and his wife knew not what to do about this, for every time the mare gave birth, by morning the foal would be gone.

One May Eve, Teyrnon said to his wife, "By God, I shall surely find out what happens to those foals." And so he armed himself and had the mare brought into the house where he could watch over her. Once night had fallen, the mare dropped a fine, black foal. It was a sturdy little thing, and got to its feet immediately.

No sooner did the foal stand up but a long black arm burst through the window and grabbed the foal by its mane. Teyrnon drew his sword and slashed at the arm, cutting it off at the elbow. A terrible scream sounded from outside, and another noise that Teyrnon could not identify. He ran to the door to find out what the noise was, and there on the step he found a golden-haired baby boy, swaddled tightly in silken swaddling clothes that were richly embroidered.

Teyrnon picked up the child and brought it to his wife. "My wife, wake up. For here I have a son for you, if you want him."

Then Teyrnon told her the whole story. When he was done, she looked at the boy and saw how he was dressed. "Surely this is the son of some nobleman," she said. "If we are to keep him, we must first send out news that I was with child, and get our serving-women to say the same."

Teyrnon agreed, and it was done as his wife said. They took the boy into their home and raised him as his own. They had him baptized and named him Gwri Wallt Euryn, because he had golden hair. The boy grew quickly and well, and by the time he was a year old he had the growth and strength of a three year old. At the end of his second year, he was as big and strong as a six year old. By the time he was four, he wished to be allowed to work in the stables and care for the horses.

One day, Teyrnon's wife came to him and asked what had happened to the foal that was born the night they found their son.

"I told the stable hands to care for it," said Teyrnon.

"Perhaps it is time that it be trained, and then given to our son?" said his wife.

Teyrnon agreed, and so the horse was trained to carry a rider and given to Gwri for his own.

Soon after this, word of what had happened to Rhiannon and her punishment came to the court of Teyrnon. He listened to the tales carefully and felt sorry for the woman. He also looked very closely at Gwri and realized that the boy resembled Pwyll in every feature. Teyrnon knew Pwyll by sight, for once Pwyll had owed him fealty.

Teyrnon realized that he could not rightfully keep the boy, and this grieved him, for he loved Gwri well. But he knew that the boy must be returned to his rightful parents, and that Rhiannon must be freed from her unjust punishment, so he went to his wife and told her what he intended. Teyrnon's wife listened to all her husband said and agreed that bringing Gwri to the court of Pwyll was the proper thing to do.

The next day Teyrnon and Gwri set out for Pwyll's court with two noble companions. When they arrived at the gate, Rhiannon rose and said, "Stay, for it is my punishment for having killed my own son that I should carry each of you on my back into the court."

"Nay, lady," said Teyrnon, "that you'll not do, for me, or for any who are with me."

Gwri also said that he would not let Rhiannon carry him, and the nobles said likewise. Teyrnon, Gwri, and their companions then went into the court of Pwyll, and they were given a warm welcome. Pwyll ordered a feast be prepared for them, and when the tables were ready Teyrnon sat between Pwyll and Rhiannon, and his two nobles above them with the boy Gwri between them.

After the feast was over, Teyrnon told his story about the foal and about the boy. He explained how he had taken the boy in to foster, and how he and his wife had raised him as their own.

"But when we heard the tale of Rhiannon's punishment," said Teyrnon, "we sorrowed greatly for it. We then realized that our Gwri must be your son indeed. If you look at the boy, it is clear that he could be no man's son save Pwyll's. We now return him to you, his rightful parents."

"How my cares would be lightened if what you say is true," said Rhiannon.

And all the nobles of the court looked at the boy and at Pwyll, and all agreed that the boy must be Pwyll's son.

"And what is his name?" asked one of Pwyll's nobles.

"We call him Gwri Wallt Euryn, but you may name him as you wish," said Teyrnon.

"Pryderi shall be his name," said Pwyll, "for that name means 'care,' and this was the first thing his mother said about him upon meeting him."

Rhiannon and Pwyll and the nobles agreed that this was a fine name for the boy, and so he was known as Pryderi son of Pwyll Pen Annwfn ever after.

Then Pwyll turned to Teyrnon and said, "By God, I know no way to compensate you for the good upbringing you have given our son. But when he is grown, surely he will repay you in a fitting manner."

"My lord," said Teyrnon, "you should know that no one grieves for the loss of the boy than does my wife, who loves him as a mother. He should remember her thus; that is my wish."

Pwyll then promised that Pryderi would never forget Teyrnon and his wife, nor the care they had given him when he was a child. And Pwyll promised to ally himself and his realm with Teyrnon and his domain, and that Pryderi would do the same after him. Then the boy was given to the nobleman Pendaran Dyfed to foster, but Pwyll also made Teyrnon and his nobles foster fathers as well.

When it was time for Teyrnon and his companions to leave, Pwyll and Rhiannon offered Teyrnon many fine gifts of gold and silver and costly jewels, and of the best horses they had. But Teyrnon would accept none of those, and he departed Pwyll's court much contented all the same.

And so Pryderi was brought up at the court of Pwyll Pen Annwfn, and soon there was none in all the land to match him for good looks or strength of body or deeds. And when Pwyll grew aged and died, Pryderi became the prince of Dyfed, and he conquered the three cantrefs, or counties, of Ystrad Tywi and the four cantrefs of Ceredigion besides. Pryderi took to himself a noble wife, and together they ruled wisely and well to the end of their days.

The Story of Culhwch and Olwen

In his edition of the Mabinogion, *Patrick Ford notes the importance of horses at the birth of Gwri/Pryderi in the story of Pwyll of Dyfed, while in the story of Culhwch the animals involved are pigs. Ford traces these respectively to the Celtic horse-goddess Epona and the pig-god Moccus. By the time these stories were written down, these deities exist only as mere echoes, in the association of horses and pigs with the births of boy-heroes. Moccus also would appear to be represented in Culhwch's story by the monstrous boar Twrch Trwyth, who must be hunted and destroyed by King Arthur and his companions.*

It is important to note that this is not quite the King Arthur that we are familiar with today. The Arthur of this tale is an earlier manifestation, one who exists in the realm of ancient Celtic myth and legend. Only later was he adopted as a Christianized hero-king and literary figure by medieval court culture, which is the more common source for modern retellings of Arthurian legends.

Once there was a prince of Wales named Cilydd, son of Celyddon, and he took to wife Goleuddydd, daughter of Prince Anlawdd. Cilydd's people rejoiced at this marriage, for it was a very good match, and they prayed that soon their prince might have a son and heir. They had not long to wait before their prayers were answered: Goleuddydd soon found herself with child.

All was not easy with Goleuddydd, however. She found that she could not abide being indoors, and so she went wandering about the countryside, never returning to her home and even sleeping under the stars or beneath the trees. When she felt it was close to the time for her to be delivered, she looked for shelter. There on the side of a mountain she found the abode of a swineherd. She went into the swineherd's hut, but she found the pigs so frightening that she immediately gave birth. She named the boy Culhwch, which means "place of the pigs," because that was where he was born. The swineherd recognized Goleuddydd, so when she was well enough to travel he returned her with her baby to the court of Prince Cilydd that the boy might be brought up amongst his own people, for not only was Culhwch the son of Cilydd, he also was cousin to King Arthur himself.

Culhwch grew quickly and well, but when he was still quite a small child his mother grew ill and died. When Goleuddydd was on her deathbed, she told Cilydd, "I know that you soon will wish to remarry, but I worry that your new bride will try to disinherit our son, Culhwch. I ask that you not take another wife until you see a briar with two blossoms upon it on my grave. I also bid that you tend my grave well and not neglect it."

Prince Cilydd promised Goleuddydd that she would do all that she asked him, and after she died and was buried he appointed a servant to tend the grave and keep it free from any kind of weed or briar. For seven years, the servant did his task well, but after that time he tired of it, and so the grave went untended.

It was at this time that the prince rode out to hunt, and bethought himself to visit the grave of Goleuddydd to see whether there might be anything growing upon it. He went to the place where she was buried and saw that a briar had begun growing in the middle of her grave, and upon that briar were two blossoms. The prince returned to his palace and summoned to him his wisest advisers. He asked them whether they knew of any well-born woman who might serve as a new wife.

"Yes," said one. "The wife of King Doged would do admirably."

Cilydd agreed that this was good advice. He sent a party of his choicest warriors to Doged's lands. There they killed Doged and captured his wife and daughter. They also scoured the towns and villages of that place and took their plunder back to Cilydd's domain. Cilydd took possession of Doged's lands, and took his widow to be his own wife, but Cilydd told her nothing about Culhwch, for he had not forgotten Goleuddydd's dying words to him about their son.

One day, Cilydd's new wife went for a walk through the countryside. She came upon a crude hut, in front of which sat an old woman with straggly white hair and but one tooth in her mouth. Now, Cilydd's wife had heard tales of this woman, and knew that she had a reputation for soothsaying. Cilydd's wife also had many questions about her new husband, questions she knew would be unwise to ask at court. She therefore approached the old woman and said, "Tell me, old woman, how is it that I have wed a childless man? Will I not have an heir by him?"

The old woman said, "Cilydd is not childless, and you are assured of producing an heir of your own body."

"Tell me of this child that Cilydd has," said the wife, for she was surprised to hear that her husband had been keeping this a secret.

"Cilydd has one son," said the old woman, "and his name is Culhwch."

Cilydd's wife returned home. She went straight to her husband and demanded to know why he had been keeping his son a secret from her. At first Cilydd tried to evade her questions, but finally he summoned Culhwch to him and presented the boy to his new stepmother. She looked the boy up and down and saw that he was handsome and well made in his body.

"You are a fine-looking lad," said his stepmother, "and you should think of marriage. I myself have a beautiful daughter who would make an excellent wife for you."

Culhwch replied, "That may be so, but I am not yet of an age to take a wife."

This angered his stepmother, and so she pronounced a curse upon him: "If you take not my daughter, then never shall you wed, except it be to Olwen, daughter of Ysbaddaden Pencawr, king of the giants!"

At this, Culhwch felt his whole body overcome with love for Olwen, a woman he had never met, and he vowed to himself that he would take her to wife.

Cilydd saw that the lad was blushing strangely, and asked, "What is the matter, my son? Have you taken ill?"

"No," said Culhwch, "but I have heard the fate foretold me by my stepmother, and I wish to see whether I might have the hand of Olwen, daughter of Ysbaddaden Pencawr, in marriage."

Cilydd said, "That should not be difficult for you, for you are nobly born and cousin to King Arthur himself. You should go to the court of Arthur and ask him for his aid in this matter. Tidy yourself, and get your hair cut, and then go and speak to Arthur."

The next morning, Culhwch set out for Arthur's court. He rode a fine grey steed, and his saddle and bridle were inlaid with much gold. Culhwch was richly dressed and armed with spear and sword in a manner befitting a prince, and he carried a fine hunting horn that was chased with silver. At Culhwch's side coursed two of the best hunting hounds, wearing golden collars inlaid with rubies. And the tread of Culhwch's mount was so light that it did not even bend the grass beneath his hooves as they cantered to the court of King Arthur.

When Culhwch reached the court of King Arthur, he found the gate closed and barred.

"Let me in," Culhwch said to the sentry.

"I cannot," said the sentry, "for the feast has already begun, and it is Arthur's law that none be allowed to enter save those who have been specially invited. But here outside the wall there is a guesthouse, where there is food and drink aplenty and a warm bed fit even for a noble prince, and stabling for your horse and your hounds. You may stay here the night, and seek audience of Arthur in the morning."

"I'll not wait," said Culhwch, "and if you open not the gate, I shall send up three shouts. The first shall be heard throughout all of Wales. The second shall be heard as far away as Ireland. And the third shall be so loud and so fierce that all the women in the land who now are with child shall miscarry, and those who are now barren shall remain so forevermore."

"Shout as you might," said the sentry, "I cannot unbar this gate save by permission of the king. I bid you wait while I ask him what I should do."

The sentry went into the hall where King Arthur sat a-feasting with his court. The king saw the sentry, and bid him say what had brought him into the hall.

"A warrior there is at the gate," said the sentry, "the likes of which I have never seen, neither for raiment, nor weapons, nor steed, nor hounds, nor for good looks, nor strength of body. As you well know, I have travelled to every land, to India, to Africa, to Norway, and to Greece, and all the places in between, and never have I seen such a youth as this. He craves audience with Your Majesty, and says he will not wait. I am here to ask whether I may admit him, despite your law."

Arthur said, "Surely such a man as this ought not to be kept waiting. I waive the law of the banquet hall for this special guest. Bid him enter, and make him welcome."

Then Kai, one of the knights of the king said, "If Your Majesty pleases, I counsel that we not admit this man to our feast in defiance of the law."

Arthur replied, "I cannot take your counsel, my friend, for if I refuse this warrior entrance, it will bring great shame upon me and upon this court."

No sooner had Arthur said this, than Culhwch strode into the banqueting hall. All who saw him marveled, for the sentry's description had not done him justice. Arthur welcomed Culhwch warmly, and invited him to take a seat at table, where meat and wine would be brought to him.

"I come not for the feast," said Culhwch, "but to beg the aid of Your Majesty. And if you give me not your aid, great will be the shame upon you and upon your court."

"All that I have to give is yours," said Arthur, "save my weapons, and my ship, and my cloak, and my wife."

"First I wish that you should cut my hair," said Culhwch.

Arthur called for a comb and scissors to be brought. Culhwch was then seated before the king, and as Arthur combed and trimmed Culhwch's hair, he said, "Tell me now who you are, and of your family."

"I am Culhwch, son of Cilydd son of Celyddon, and my mother was Goleuddydd, daughter of Prince Anlawdd."

"Ah!" said Arthur. "Then we are cousins, surely. Doubly welcome you are to my court, kinsman. Now tell me what it is you require of me."

"I wish to wed Olwen, daughter of Ysbaddaden Pencawr, king of the giants," said Culhwch. "I beg your assistance in finding her and making her my bride."

Arthur admitted that he did not know who this young woman might be. Neither did any of his courtiers know of her, so Arthur pledged to send messengers throughout his kingdom to see where she might be found. Culhwch agreed that it should be done thus, and gave Arthur a year in which to find the girl.

And so the year passed, without any of the messengers being able to find Olwen or her people. Culhwch came before the court and said to Arthur, "I can wait no longer. If you can be of no help to me, then I must go on this quest by myself."

"Not so," said Kai, "for I will come with you."

"Yes," said Arthur. "It is wise that you take Kai as your companion. Also I will send others of my finest warriors, so that you will always have the best help."

Arthur called upon Kai and five others to be Culhwch's companions. Each of these was a fearsome warrior, and each had other qualities and skills besides. Kai could hold his breath under water for nine days and nine nights, and he could go without sleep for the same space. If he wounded someone with his sword, that wound would never heal no matter how well it was tended. Kai could make himself grow until he was as tall as a tree, and with his body he could make enough heat that the rain could not touch whatever he carried, and even could start a fire with that heat.

Bedwyr One-Hand also went with Culhwch. Bedwyr was the fastest man in the kingdom. No one could match him for speed, save Arthur and one other, a man named Drych Ail Cybdar. Although Bedwyr had only one hand, he was as deadly in battle as three two-handed men, and his lance was so deadly that any wound made with it would be nine times greater than the lance of another warrior.

Cynddelig Cyfarwydd the guide also was summoned to go with Culhwch. No one knew the lands in Arthur's realm better than he, and none was his match at finding a path through unknown lands. The interpreter Gwyrhyr Gwstad Ieithoedd also was part of the company, for he spoke all languages, and Gwalchmai mab Gwyar also joined them, for he was the best horseman and the best fighter on foot. The last member of the company was Menw son of Teirgwaedd, who could cast a spell of invisibility about himself and his companions, so that unfriendly eyes could not see them.

Culhwch and his companions set out from Arthur's castle and travelled until they came to a wide plain. On the plain, far in the distance, was a castle the like of which they had never seen. The plain was so wide that it took them three days to cross it. When they finally neared the castle, they found an enormous flock of sheep between themselves and the castle. The shepherd was a huge, fearsome-looking man, sitting on a hillock near his flock, and next to him was a giant sheepdog, as large as a horse. What was more, the shepherd could throw flames out of his mouth at anyone who displeased him, and many charred trees and shrubs were all about.

Kai, Gwyrhyr, and Menw decided among themselves to speak to the shepherd. Menw said that he would cast a charm on him so that they might speak with him safely. The three companions strode up to the shepherd. "Greetings," they said to him. "Tell us, if you will, who you are, and who is master of that castle, and of all these fine sheep?"

"My name is Custennin, and surely everyone knows whose castle and whose herds these are," said the shepherd. "They belong to Ysbaddaden Pencawr, king of the giants. Why do you ask? What do you want here?"

"We are messengers from the court of King Arthur," said Kai, "and we are come to ask the hand of Olwen in marriage for one of our companions."

"Oh," said the shepherd, "I pity your friend and all your companions, if that truly is your errand. Many suitors have come to this land asking for the hand of Olwen, and not one has ever left here alive."

Culhwch thanked the shepherd for what he had told them, and gave him a golden ring as payment. The shepherd tried to put on the ring, but it would not fit his huge fingers, so he put it inside his glove and took it home to his wife. When he gave her the ring, she said, "Where did you find such a thing, husband?"

"I went to the shore to do some fishing, and there I found a dead man on the beach. The ring was on his hand, so I took it."

"A likely story," said the wife. "Show me this fine corpse that wears beautiful jewelry."

"Never fear," said Custennin. "You shall see him shortly. In fact, he and his friends likely will be here soon, to ask us for our hospitality for the night."

"Whatever do you mean?" said the wife.

"I mean that it is Culhwch, son of Cilydd son of Celyddon, whose mother was Goleuddydd daughter of Anlawdd, who is here. He is come to ask for the hand of Olwen in marriage."

The shepherd's wife was both happy and sad at this news. She was happy, because Culhwch was her sister's son, and sad because she knew that no one ever returned from the castle of Ysbyddaden Pencawr alive. But she had not time to dwell on this, because soon she heard the sounds of Culhwch and his companions approaching. She ran out to greet them and went to embrace the companions. First she went to Kai, but before she could touch him, Kai grabbed a huge log from the woodpile and thrust it between himself and the woman. The woman embraced the log instead, and soon it was nothing but a pile of splinters.

"It is fortunate that it was not I you embraced," said Kai.

The woman invited the companions into her house and provided them with food and drink. Then she went over to the fireplace, and opened a door that stood next to the mantelpiece. Behind the door was a small, secret room, and out of the secret room came a beautiful youth, who had curly, golden hair.

"What has he done, to be imprisoned in that room so?" said Gwrhyr.

"It is to save him that he hides in that secret room," said the wife. "Twenty-four sons I once had, and now all of them are dead save

51

him. All the others were slain by Ysbaddaden Pencawr, and our only hope to keep this one alive is to hide him."

"Let him stay with me," said Kai. "I swear I shall protect him, and none shall harm him save they kill me first."

When the meal was finished, the shepherd's wife asked, "Tell me, now: why have you come here, and what is it you seek?"

"We come to seek the hand of Olwen for our friend Culhwch," said Kai.

"That is most unwise," said the woman. "If you value your lives, leave now, before anyone from the castle can see you."

"We will not," said Kai, "at least, not until we have seen the maiden."

"Is there a place she goes where we might see her without being seen?" said Gwrhyr.

"Yes," said the woman. "She comes here every Saturday to wash her hair. When she does, she puts one of her rings into a dish. She always forgets to take them back afterwards, and no one from the castle ever comes to get them, either. She comes tomorrow on this errand, and I will let you see her without yourselves being seen, but only if you promise to do her no harm."

Culhwch and his companions agreed that this was a good plan, and they made solemn promises not to harm the maiden.

The next morning, Olwen came to wash her hair. She wore a gown of silk, red as flame, and around her neck was a torc of red gold, studded with many gems. Her hair was shining gold, her skin whiter than milk, and her eyes brighter than those of the swiftest falcon. Wherever she trod upon the grass, white clover flowers would spring up, and it is for this reason she was called Olwen, which means "White Track."

As soon as Culhwch saw her, he stepped forward and said, "Lady, I greet you well, for I have always loved you. Come with me, for I would have you as my bride."

"I must not wed you," said Olwen, "not without my father's consent, because the moment I am wed, he will die. Instead I ask you to go to his castle and beg an audience with him. Whatever he asks you to do, agree to it without hesitation, for if you do what he asks then maybe he will allow us to marry. But do not hesitate, whatever he asks, otherwise he will kill you instantly."

"This I shall do," said Culhwch.

The next day, Culhwch and his companions set out for the castle where they had to go through nine gates. At each gate was a gatekeeper with a giant mastiff. Culhwch and his companions slew each gatekeeper with his dog, marched through each gate, and soon found themselves in the hall of Ysbyddaden Pencawr, king of the giants.

"Who are you, and what do you want?" roared Ysbyddaden.

"We are here to ask the hand of your daughter Olwen in marriage to our companion, Culhwch son of Cilydd," said Kai.

"Where are my servants?" said Ysbyddaden. "Bring me the forks that hold up my eyelids, so that I can see this young fool who thinks to wed my daughter."

The servants brought the forks and placed them under the giant's eyelids. He looked Culhwch up and down. "So, you think to marry my Olwen, eh?" he said. "Come back tomorrow. You will have my answer then."

The companions turned to go, but as they did so, Ysbyddaden grasped one of the three poisoned spears that he kept behind his throne, and hurled it at Culhwch. But before the spear could find its mark, Bedwyr caught it in midair and flung it back at the giant. The spear struck Ysbyddaden in the knee, and he howled with pain. "I shall never be able to walk properly again!" he cried.

The companions returned to Custennin's house, where they feasted and rejoiced that they had survived their first encounter with the giant. The next day, they rose early and dressed and groomed themselves with care, so that they would look their very best when next they spoke to Ysbyddaden.

Again they went into the hall of the king of the giants. This time Gwrhyr spoke for the company.

"Give us Olwen to be the bride of Culhwch, and in exchange we will give you the usual dowry, plus gifts for you and for her kinswomen. But if you do not give her to us, you will die."

"You must wait for my answer," said Ysbyddaden, "for all of her great-grandparents are still alive, and I must ask their advice first."

"Very well," said Gwrhyr. "We shall go and eat while you speak with them."

Again the companions turned to go, and again Ysbyddaden threw a poisoned spear at Culhwch. This time Menw it was who caught the spear and hurled it back. So fierce and strong was Menw's cast that the spear went straight through the giant, at the middle of his breast. "Alas!" cried the giant, "now I shall always have chest pains and indigestion!"

The companions returned to Custennin's house, where they ate and spent the night. In the morning, they returned to the giant's hall.

"Throw not another spear at us, O Giant," said Kai, "else you risk being killed by us!"

At this Ysbyddaden called for the servants to put the forks under his eyelids so that he could see, and when this was done he grabbed the last spear and hurled it at Culhwch. This time it was Culhwch himself who caught the spear and flung it back, and it went straight into the giant's eye and came out the back of his neck. "Alas!" cried the giant, "now I shall have headaches forever, and my eye will always weep when I have to walk outside on a windy day!"

The companions again returned to the shepherd's house, and on the morrow went back to the giant's hall.

"Do not turn us away, O Giant," said Kai, "and do not throw any more spears at us, or we will surely kill you! Give us your daughter, to be the bride of Culhwch."

"Which one of you is Culhwch?" said Ysbyddaden.

Culhwch stepped forward. "I am Culhwch," he said.

"Come here and sit with me, so that we may discuss this matter," said the giant.

Culhwch went and sat with him.

"So, you have come to ask the hand of my daughter in marriage, yes?" said Ysbyddaden.

"Yes, I am," said Culhwch.

"First you must promise that you will always be entirely honest with me," said Ysbyddaden.

"I pledge honesty to you gladly," said Culhwch.

"Then I will give you my daughter, if you can do the deeds I command of you."

"You have but to ask," said Culhwch.

At this the giant named one task after another, each of them difficult and dangerous. Culhwch was to clear and plow a field that could not be plowed; he had to obtain a magic drinking-horn and a magic harp; he had to make a magic leash from the hairs of a beard of a fearsome warrior, because that was the only thing that would hold the hound Culhwch was to find; he had to get the sword of Wrnach the giant, and many other tasks besides. But the most difficult, dangerous, and important task was to get the comb, shears, and razor that rested between the ears of the giant boar Twrch Trwyth.

After each task Culhwch said, "It will be no trouble for me to do that." And after the very last task was named he said, "It will be no trouble to do any of that, for my kinsman Arthur will give me all the help I need."

Culhwch and his companions returned to the court of King Arthur. Not only did Arthur pledge his warriors to help accomplish everything Ysbyddaden had commanded, he himself went on the quest, as did the golden-haired son of Custennin the Shepherd, whose name was Goreu.

Up and down the country went Arthur and his warriors, easily achieving everything Ysbaddaden had commanded, and they returned to Celli Weg in Cornwall, from where they would begin the task of getting the comb, shears, and razor from between the ears of Twrch Trwyth. Arthur called for Menw son of Teirgwaedd and said to him, "Go and look for Twrch Trwyth, and see whether the treasures are indeed between his ears. For I would not have us waste time and effort looking for him, if what we seek is not there."

Menw learned that the boar was in Ireland, so he went there to look for him. Soon enough, he found the boar's lair, and Menw caught a glimpse of the three treasures as the boar went inside. Menw turned himself in to a bird and waited. When the boar came out, Menw swooped down and tried to snatch one of the treasures, but he only managed to grasp a clawful of bristles. This enraged Twrch Trwyth, and he shook himself, sending poison flying from his hide. Some of the poison landed on Menw, and he was marked by it ever after.

Upon learning where the boar was, and that he did indeed have the three treasures, Arthur gathered a great company of warriors from as far away as Brittany. He also called to him all the finest hunting steeds and the finest coursing hounds, and soon he had such a mighty army that when he landed, the Irish were in great fear of him, and sent their holy men to treat with him and ask his protection upon them. Arthur agreed to this gladly, and the holy men provided him and his army with food.

Arthur and his army went to Esgair Oerfel, which is where the boar had his home, along with his seven young pigs. They loosed the hounds upon the boar and his brood. The Irish fought with them for the whole day, but to no avail, and a fifth of the country of Ireland was laid waste in the battle. The next day Arthur's army went with his army to fight the boar, and they fared little better. The day after that, Arthur himself went to fight with Twrch Trwyth. They fought for nine days and nine nights, and at the end of that battle only a single young pig had been killed.

When Arthur returned to camp after his fight, his men asked him, "Who is Twrch Trwyth?"

"He used to be a king," said Arthur, "but God changed him into a boar, as punishment for his sins."

Arthur called to him Gwrhyr Gwstad Ieithoedd and and told him to go and try to talk to the boar. Gwrhyr turned himself into a bird. He flew over to the place where Twrch Trwyth lived with is brood, and he perched on a nearby branch.

"In the name of God," said Gwrhyr, "if any of you can speak, I ask you to come out and talk to Arthur."

The young boar Grugyn Gwrych Eraint came forward. All of his bristles were like silver, and indeed the sparkle of them could be seen from far away. Grugyn said, "By the name of the One who put us into this form, we will not speak with Arthur, nor will we give him any help. Can you not see that we suffer enough as it is, without also being beset by Arthur and his warriors?"

Gwrhyr replied, "I must tell you that Arthur means to have the comb and shears and razor that are between the ears of Twrch Trwyth, and that he will fight for them."

"Then Arthur must come and fight," said Grugyn, "for Twrch Trwyth will never willingly part with his treasures while he is alive. But know this: tomorrow we leave for Arthur's lands, and wherever we go shall be laid waste."

Twrch Trwyth and his brood then set out across the sea for Wales, and came ashore at Porth Clais in Dyfed. Arthur followed along in his ship, Prydwen, and however he and his warriors chased the family of boars, they could come no closer to them, until finally they held him at bay in Cwm Cerwyn. There was a great fight, and Twrch Trwyth killed four of Arthur's finest warriors. Then another four came to fight with him, and the boar himself was wounded, although in the end those four warriors perished also at the tusks of Twrch Trwyth.

The next day, Arthur's men pursued Twrch Trwyth, and wherever they managed to hold him at bay, he slew them all. Twrch Trwyth ran all the way to Glyn Ystun, and it was there that Arthur's men lost him.

Arthur then called to him Gwyn son of Nudd. He asked whether Gwyn knew anything that might help them hunt and kill Twrch Trwyth, but Gwyn said that he did not. The men finally picked up the trail of the great boar and his brood. They hunted them up and down the country, setting the hounds on them and turning them to bay, only to have the boar and the young pigs kill the hunters and get away. Finally all but Twrch Trwyth and two of his sons were killed. They separated, and the hunters pursued them in different directions. One young pig went to Ceredigion, where he slew many of the hunters but finally was brought down. Another young pig went to Ystrad Yw, and the same thing happened there.

The track of Twrch Trwyth himself was leading towards Cornwall.

"By God," said Arthur, "I'll not let that boar get into Cornwall. This chase has gone on long enough. Let us but find him and will fight him myself."

So a band of picked men went to block the path of Twrch Trwyth and turn him back to where Arthur was waiting. They caught up with the great boar, and forced him into the River Hafren. Many warriors pursued the boar into the water on their horses. The men grabbed Twrch Trwyth by the feet and held him so that he was under the water. Mabon son of Modron drew alongside the boar and grabbed the razor from him. Cyledyr Wyllt drew along the other side and snatched the shears. But before anyone could get the comb, Twrch Trwyth managed to get purchase on the bed of the river and kick his way free. He surged out of the water, and then ran so fast that neither horse nor hound could draw close to him, and in this way he reached Cornwall.

Arthur and his men pursued Twrch Trwyth throughout Cornwall. When they finally cornered the beast, there was a terrific fight the likes of which had never been seen before, and which was fiercer than any they had had with the boar since they first started chasing him. But after this fight, Arthur finally managed to snatch the comb. Twrch Trwyth turned tail and ran. He came to the shore, where he did not stop but instead ran straight into the sea, and he was never seen nor heard from again after that.

Arthur returned to where Culhwch was waiting, having won all the treasures that Ysbyddaden required. Then they set out for the giant's court. Goreu son of Custennin the Shepherd went with them, for he had cause to hate Ysbyddaden for killing all his brothers and making him live a prisoner's life.

They reached the court of Ysbyddaden, and showed him all the things they had achieved. Then Caw of Prydyn took the comb and shears and razor of Twrch Trwyth and shaved Ysbyddaden. He shaved the giant's beard, and his flesh straight down to the bone, and his ears as well.

And Culhwch said, "Have you been thoroughly shaven?"

Ysbyddaden replied, "That I have."

"And is your daughter now free to be my bride?" said Culhwch.

"That she is," said the giant. "But do not thank me for it, but rather Arthur, for it is by his deeds that you have her at all. If it had been left to me, you never would have had her. And now it is time to put an end to me."

At that Goreu son of Custennin took the giant by the hair and struck off his head. Then he fixed the head to a post at the gate of the castle, and took for himself all the giant's lands and possessions. Arthur and all his warriors returned to their own lands. Culhwch wed Olwen, and they were happily married to the end of their days.

And that is the tale of how Culhwch won Olwen.

PART II
Cornwall and Brittany

The Drowned City of Ys

This story from Brittany places ancient Celtic elements, such as druidesses and Otherworldly creatures, within the struggle of the old Celtic faith against the spread of Christianity. We have already seen this conflict in the Irish tale of the Children of Lir, which casts the children first as tragic victims of Christianization and then later converts to that religion. In the present tale, however, the character of Dahut, who is the product of the union between a human king and an Otherworldly sea maiden, is drawn as wicked, murderous, and willfully opposed to Christianity. Whereas the Children of Lir ultimately are saved through the actions of Christians, Dahut brings about her own downfall and that of the City of Ys when she consorts with a stranger who likely represents the Christian Devil.

Once, long ago, there was a great city in Brittany called Ys. No one today knows exactly where it was, for it was lost beneath the sea. Some say that the ruins of Ys lie in the Baie de Trepasses. Some say that they lie in the Baie de Douarnenez. But wherever the city may lie, on some nights those who live on the coast of Brittany hear the bells of Ys ringing out ghostly across the waters of the sea. And when the people hear those bells, they shiver, and think of the tale of how the city was built, and how it was lost, all those many years ago.

The tale begins in the kingdom of Cornouaille, which was ruled by King Gradlon. Gradlon was a wise and generous king. He always tried to rule justly, and he worshiped the old gods, for Christianity had not yet come to that part of France. Gradlon had but one daughter, whose name was Dahut. She had skin as pale as ivory, eyes as dark as coals, and long black hair that flowed like a river. Dahut's mother had come from the sea, having fallen in love with the handsome, kingly Gradlon from afar. The sea-maiden enchanted the king one day, so that he took her to wife, but then he displeased her, and so she returned to the sea and was never seen again. But before she left, she bore Gradlon a daughter, and Gradlon loved Dahut more than anything else in the world, for she reminded him of her mother, his lost queen.

One day, Gradlon and some of his courtiers went hunting in the forest of Menez-Hom where the hounds flushed out a great wild boar. Gradlon and his courtiers spurred their mounts to the chase. They raced through stands of trees and across streams. They pushed through thickets and bounded over fallen logs. But no matter how hard the hunters rode, and no matter how swiftly the hounds coursed after the boar, they could not catch it.

Finally, Gradlon called a halt to the chase. The hounds and the horses were spent, and so were the hunters. As they paused to catch their breath, the men looked about them and realized they had no idea where they were. They had been so intent on following the boar that they had paid no attention to the path they had taken. They were utterly lost, in a part of the forest none of them had ever seen before, and the sun was beginning to set.

"Let us head in that direction," said one of the courtiers, pointing towards the west. "I am certain we crossed a stream there, and at the very least we can water the animals while we decide what to do next."

Gradlon agreed that this was wise advice, so the king and his companions turned towards the west and went slowly towards the place where the courtier thought the stream had been. They rode for some minutes with no sign of a stream, but then they came upon a clearing in which was a small hut, with a well nearby. One of the courtiers dismounted and went to the hut. In answer to his knock, a man in a monk's habit came to the door.

"Welcome to my hermitage," said the monk. "My name is Corentin. How may I serve you?"

"Greetings," said the courtier. "We are a party of hunters who have become lost in the forest. We saw your hut, and have come to ask whether you might direct us back to the city of Quimper. For the leader of our party is Gradlon, king of Cornouaille."

"Certainly," said Corentin. "I will be pleased to help His Majesty and all of you get home safely. But I see that you have had a long and tiring hunt, and your animals are spent. May I offer you hospitality, so that you might refresh yourselves and your animals before you travel on?"

Gradlon and his courtiers gratefully accepted Corentin's invitation. First Corentin spread a beautiful white cloth on the clean, soft grass in front of his hut for Gradlon to sit upon. Then he went into his hut and fetched out a large basket and a large flagon. While some of the courtiers tended to the horses and hounds, others followed Corentin to the well, where first he filled the flagon with clear water. Then he plunged his hand into the well and brought out a little fish. He cut the fish in half with a knife he carried on his belt. One half of the fish he put into the basket, while the other he tossed back into the well. The courtiers looked where the piece had fallen into the well and were amazed to see that the little fish once again was whole.

Corentin returned to the place where Gradlon was sitting, carrying the flagon and the basket. When he put these down upon the white cloth, the basket immediately became full of all the choicest foods, and the flagon with the best red wine. Gradlon and his courtiers feasted on all the good things that came from the basket. There was plenty for all, and enough to satisfy the hounds besides. The king pronounced the wine the finest he had ever tasted and, what was more, no matter how much the companions and their host drank, the flagon was always full, and no one became drunk.

During the meal, Corentin and Gradlon conversed together. Corentin told the king and his courtiers of the Gospels and the ways of the Christian faith, answering every question that was put to him. Gradlon found Corentin to be a wise and learned man. He listened carefully and well to everything the hermit had to say. By the end of the meal, Gradlon and his courtiers had decided to become Christians, and Corentin baptized them with water from the well.

Soon it was time for Gradlon and his companions to depart. "Come with me back to Quimper," the king said to Corentin. "Your wisdom and teachings are sorely needed there."

At first Corentin was reluctant, because he loved his little hermitage in the woods. But then he decided to go with the king, for he realized there was much work for him to do in bringing the Gospel to the people of Cornouaille. Under Corentin's guidance, many of the king's subjects converted to Christianity, and churches were built all across Quimper.

Gradlon was well pleased with the spread of the new faith, as were his courtiers and many of his subjects, and especially Corentin, who had not expected to meet with such success. Dahut, however, became unhappy and withdrawn. She kept to her chamber, and often seemed to be weeping. When she was not in her chamber, she was at the top of the westernmost tower of the palace, where she would sit looking out in the direction of the sea.

One day Gradlon noticed how sickly Dahut looked. "My daughter," he said, "will you not tell me what it is that troubles you so?"

Dahut replied, "Quimper is no longer hospitable to me. There are churches everywhere now. The churches are full of priests and monks who can do nothing but chant without ceasing, even when they go about in the streets. The bells that rang for the old festivals no longer sound, and instead we hear bells for the new faith. The old gods have been forsaken. Joy is gone from the world."

"What can I do to ease your pain?" said Gradlon.

"Build for me a city by the sea," said Dahut, "for I feel it always calling to me. I think I would be happy again if I could live where I could see the waves and feel their spray, and smell the salt of the water."

Gradlon agreed that it should be done as Dahut asked. He caused a great city of stone to be built on the coast, with elegant houses whose walls were paneled with cedar and with real glass panes in the windows. Gradlon also ordered a new palace to be built there, so that betimes he could join his daughter when his duties in Quimper permitted.

When the city was finished, it was given the name of Ys. The City of Ys prospered, for it was soon filled with merchants and artisans who traded far and wide, and fishermen who plied the waters of the bay to feed the inhabitants. But for all its splendor, the City of Ys contained not a single church of the new faith.

Dahut was delighted with the new city. Within a few days of living there, her former health and good humor returned. Gradlon himself soon found that living there was so pleasant that he moved his court to Ys, and there he dwelled in the new palace with Dahut, leaving Corentin to administer Quimper on his behalf as Bishop of Cornouaille.

Word that there was no church in Ys soon came to the ears of Corentin, who wrote to the king asking why he had neglected to honor the Lord with even one house of worship. Just as Gradlon was reading Corentin's letter, Dahut came to her father to discuss an important matter. She had looked out over the city, and saw that it needed a seawall to protect it from flooding if ever there were a great storm. But when she saw Corentin's letter and heard of his demand that Gradlon build a church, she fell into a rage.

"You built Ys so that I might have a place without churches and priests," Dahut said. "And now I see I shall never be free of them."

Dahut was convinced that her father would do Corentin's bidding first, and leave the seawall until later, so she decided to take matters into her own hands. That night she stole away to the beach and took a small sailboat. She sailed out to the Isle of Sein, a mysterious place off the coast from which, it was said, visitors never returned. Not only was the Isle dangerous to approach because of its many reefs and submerged rocks: also it was inhabited by nine druidesses who still practiced the old faith. It was said that these druidesses were able to change their shapes at will, and that they were served by Korrigans, a race of faerie beings who had not yet fallen victim to the new faith.

When Dahut neared the Isle, she furled the sail and bent her back to the oars. She navigated the rocks and the reefs with skill, and when the time was right, jumped out of her little boat and pulled it up onto the sand. Dahut stood on the beach for a long moment, trying to decide which way to go, when she heard the sound of women chanting. She went in the direction of the sound, which was coming from a stand of oak trees toward the center of the island. When she got closer, she saw that a fire was burning in a clearing, and around the fire were the nine druidesses, singing magical songs of the old faith. The women noticed Dahut standing there, and stopped their song.

Dahut said to them, "I am Dahut, daughter of Gradlon, king of Cornouaille. I am a follower of the old faith, and I have come to ask for your help."

The eldest woman stepped forward and said, "You are most welcome, Dahut daughter of Gradlon, and daughter of the old faith. We here are but the few who remain who still know the old ways, but what we can do to serve you we will do."

Dahut explained to them how Gradlon had built Ys for her without any Christian churches, and how he now planned to change that because of the demand of Corentin. She also told them that Ys needed a seawall, for it was built very close to the coast and was in danger of flooding, but that Gradlon planned to build the church first and thus leave the city unprotected from the sea while that was being done.

The druidesses listened carefully to Dahut's request, and agreed to help her. Using their magic, they called to them the Korrigans. The women asked the Korrigans to go to Ys and build the seawall before the night was done, but also to build a grand new palace for Dahut to live in, one that would be taller and more beautiful than any church ever could be. The Korrigans said that they would gladly build the wall and the palace for a daughter of the old faith, and then they vanished.

Dahut thanked the women for their help. Then she went back to her boat and returned to Ys. As she came within sight of the city, she saw that the seawall and new palace had already been finished. They were made out of blocks of white stone perfectly carved and polished. They reflected the moonlight in such a way that they looked as though they were glowing with a light of their own. In the seawall was a massive sluice gate, which could be controlled with a set of silver keys. Once again Dahut furled the sail of her boat and rowed toward shore. When she went through the open gate, she saw that the keys were waiting for her there in the locks, looped with a silver chain. Steadying her boat against the inside of the seawall, Dahut turned the keys, closing the sluice gate. She took the keys, and put the chain around her neck.

In the morning, Gradlon went looking for his daughter and found her in the new palace. He marveled at the new seawall and the grandeur of Dahut's new home. Gradlon asked her many times how the wall and the palace had sprung up overnight, but Dahut refused to answer him, although she gave him the keys to the sluice gate, asking him to always keep them safe.

After the seawall and the new palace were built, people came from far and wide to see the beautiful City of Ys. The city prospered greatly with new trade, and became even wealthier than it had been before. The people wore the finest clothes. They ate and drank only the choicest foods and wines. On festival days they danced the most fashionable dances, to music played by the best musicians. Soon they began to forget to attend Mass, instead preferring to spend their Sundays and holy days in feasting and revelry, until the beautiful church Gradlon had built fell into disrepair.

But above all its other charms, the City of Ys was home to the most beautiful woman in the world, Dahut, daughter of Gradlon, king of Cornouaille. Young men from all over France came to Ys in hopes of a glimpse of Dahut, and with the ambition of one day becoming her lover. Dahut encouraged this, taking one young man after another into her palace, where she would dally with them for a time, then kill them and cast their bodies into the sea when she tired of them.

Rumors began to spring up about the young men who went into the palace but never came out again. Gradlon heard these rumors, but he brushed them aside. Dahut was his beloved daughter. Surely such vile things were being said only out of jealousy of her beauty and her achievements. After all, the new prosperity of the City of Ys was entirely to her credit.

It did not take long for tales about the City of Ys and its inhabitants to reach Bishop Corentin in Quimper. Horrified by the lives of luxury the people of Ys were leading, and by their neglect of the sacred rites of the new faith, Corentin sent for the Abbot of Landevennec, a wise and humble man named Guenole. Corentin asked Guenole to go to Ys, to see what might be done to turn the people from their evil ways so that they might embrace the true faith once again.

Guenole went to Ys. He saw the people in their fine clothes dining at their great banquets. He saw the poor state of the church, its floor covered in dust so thick that small clouds of it puffed into the air with every step he took. He knew there was no time to waste, so he stood outside the church and began to preach to the people of Ys as they strode by on their daily business. Some of them stopped to listen for a little while, but did not linger, for they did not care about what Guenole had to say. Others heckled him, and still others pelted him with stale vegetables, mocking him for his humble demeanor and plain monk's habit, and for daring to tell them to reform their lives. When Abbot Guenole refused to stop preaching, the people of Ys became angry, and they chased him out of the city, threatening to kill him if he ever dared return.

Some days after the departure of Guenole, a new suitor came to Ys seeking an audience with Dahut. The suitor was tall and well built, with dark hair and dark eyes, and he rode a black horse. He wore a suit of red cloth and a heavy red cloak lined with red silk. Word came to Dahut about this handsome stranger newly arrived in the city, one more fascinating than all the rest. At first Dahut paid this no mind, for there always seemed to be no end to the stream of good-looking young men seeking her favor. But one day Dahut's maid pointed the stranger out to her, and Dahut agreed that he was unusually compelling.

Having disposed of her most recent lover the previous night, Dahut decided to hold a banquet for her suitors so that she might choose a new one to toy with, but especially that she might meet this latest arrival who was dressed all in red. At the banquet, Dahut behaved graciously to all the young men who thronged around her. She danced with all of them, and let them bring her cakes and wine. But the one who most held her attention was the stranger in red. Although he returned Dahut's courtesy, he remained aloof and did not strain himself to come to her notice.

This intrigued her all the more, so at the end of the evening, she invited him up to her private chamber.

When they arrived at her chamber, Dahut invited the stranger to make love to her, but he refused.

"Why do you refuse me this thing?" said Dahut. "A strange young man you surely must be, to scorn the favors of a beautiful young woman."

"I refuse them only because you must first do a favor for me," he replied.

"You have but to name it," said Dahut.

"Give me the keys to the sluice gate," said the stranger.

"I do not have them," said Dahut. "They are in the keeping of King Gradlon."

"Then you must go and get them," said the stranger, "for you will not have what you desire of me until I have those keys in my possession."

Dahut told the stranger to wait, and went out into the corridor. She could hear the wind rising outside, as it blew and moaned around the walls of the castle. Paying the storm no mind, Dahut crept into the chamber of the king, where he lay asleep with the keys around his neck on their silver chain. Carefully, Dahut removed the keys without waking Gradlon, and stole back to where the stranger awaited her. She gave the keys to the stranger, but instead of embracing her, he strode out of the chamber and down to the seawall, where he put the keys in the locks and opened the sluice gate. Storm-driven water soon flooded into the city.

Hearing the cries of Dahut, Gradlon awoke. He went to his daughter, then ran with her down to the stables. There they found Guenole had returned, and was waiting with two horses already saddled. The men mounted, and Gradlon pulled Dahut up behind him. They thundered through the city, the dark water swirling ever higher around the horse's hooves. But no matter how fast the king's horse galloped, it could not outrun the rising tide of the sea; the animal seemed to be hindered by a great weight.

Suddenly, the king heard the voice of Guenole calling to him over the roar of the wind and the waves:

"Throw the demon off your mount, O King! Throw her into the sea where she belongs!"

Gradlon looked behind him, but saw no demon, only his beloved daughter. His horse was tiring rapidly, and now the water was up to its hocks.

"Throw the demon off!" cried Guenole.

But Gradlon could not think what the monk meant.

"It is Dahut that holds back your mount!" said Guenole. "It is she who gave the keys to the sluice gate to her demon suitor. If you do not push her off, you will perish along with the rest of the City of Ys, for it is doomed."

Still Gradlon hesitated, but Guenole spurred his mount to run alongside the king's. Taking his staff, the monk pushed Dahut off the king's horse and into the water, where she slipped under the waves, and was never seen again. As soon as she was gone, the storm began to subside, and Gradlon's horse was able to gallop strongly again.

Gradlon and Guenole rode hard, making for higher ground. When they reached a place they thought might be safe, they turned and looked back at the City of Ys, only to see its buildings begin to crumble and fall. Then, with a great roar and rush of spray, the whole of the city sank into the sea.

There the City of Ys lies still, ruined and silent beneath the rolling waves, but on moonlit nights the faint sound of its drowned bells still can be heard ringing. And some say that at times a voice also can be heard singing, and that a young woman with skin like ivory and dark hair that flows like a river can be seen swimming gracefully under the water, ever searching for her lost palace.

The Romance of Tristan and Iseult

There are no surviving ancient Cornish myths, but the medieval story of Tristan and Iseult, which is set in Cornwall, has an analogue in "The Pursuit of Diarmuid and Grainne," an Irish story about the forbidden love between a young warrior and the bride of the king the warrior serves.

It is important to note that the word "romance" here refers not to a type of love but to a medieval literary genre known in Old French as the roman, *which often although not always involves characters engaged in* amour courtois, *or "courtly love," which is where we get many of our modern notions about romantic love. A courtly love relationship was between an unmarried knight and a lady who was married to someone else, usually the knight's lord; therefore the knight and lady were expected to remain chaste despite their feelings for one another.*

Many medieval variants of the story of Tristan and Iseult survive. The retelling below is based on the modern edition by Joseph Bernier, which was compiled from French sources.

Once there was a king in Cornwall, named Mark, and he was beset by many enemies who were trying to wrest his kingdom from him. Word of this came to Mark's friend, Rivalen, who himself was king of Lyonesse over the sea in France. Rivalen brought his army to Cornwall to help Mark. Together the two kings fought bravely alongside their soldiers, and when the war was over, Mark was victorious. In gratitude for Rivalen's courage and help, Mark gave him his sister Blanchefleur to be his wife, and Rivalen loved her well.

Blanchefleur soon was with child, but Rivalen did not live to see him born, for the king was caught in an ambush laid by Duke Morgan, who had attacked the kingdom of Lyonesse and was laying it waste. When she was told that her husband was slain, the Lady Blanchefleur gave herself up to grief, waiting only for the time when her child might be born. She soon was delivered of a fine baby boy, to whom she said, "In sorrow I have borne you, in sorrow I leave you: therefore let your name be Tristan, for that is 'child of sorrow.'" And then Blanchefleur lay back on her pillows and breathed her last.

Tristan was taken in to foster by Rivalen's marshal, Rohalt, a good man who loved his master well and who wanted to protect Rivalen's heir from Duke Morgan. He raised Tristan as his own, bringing him up well in the ways of a nobleman's son. Soon Tristan had grown into a fine young man: none could match him for strength or skill or courtesy. By evil chance was Tristan taken by pirates when he went to the harbor to look at the wares brought in by merchants from a far-off land. They were not far out to sea when a storm came up that threatened their ship. Thinking that it was their crime that had brought the storm upon them, the pirates put Tristan in a little boat and lowered it into the water. The storm immediately calmed, and the pirates sailed away. Tristan then was cast alone and friendless up onto the shores of Cornwall, where he soon fell in with some of the king's huntsmen. Tristan returned with them to Mark's court at Tintagel, where he offered himself in service to the king. Soon he became beloved of Mark and all the court, although he hid to them his parentage.

One day, Rohalt came to the court of Tintagel on an errand, and recognized his foster son. He rejoiced at seeing Tristan again, alive and whole, when he had thought him dead, and Tristan likewise was gladdened to see the man he thought of as his father. They went to Mark, and there disclosed to him the truth of Tristan's name and station. Tristan begged of Mark arms and men to avenge his father and to rid Lyonesse of the evil duke. Mark agreed, gladly, knighting Tristan himself that very day. Tristan sailed for Lyonesse on the morrow with his army, and soon they had routed the duke's men and put them to flight, while the duke himself was slain by Tristan in single combat.

Wishing to return to Mark's service, Tristan gave all his lands to Rohalt and his heirs, with the agreement of the nobles of Lyonesse. Then Tristan bade farewell to Rohalt and returned to Cornwall, taking with him only the Squire Gorvenal, who had been his master-at-arms when he was a boy.

When Tristan and Gorvenal arrived at Tintagel, they found Mark and his court in great distress. For fifteen years, the king of Ireland had demanded a heavy tribute of slaves, which Mark had refused to pay. Therefore an Irish knight named Morholt, brother of the queen of Ireland has come with his companions to tell Mark that the Irish would invade Cornwall and lay it waste unless either he paid the tribute or Morholt was defeated by a Cornish champion in single combat.

Morholt spoke his challenge boldly in the great hall of Tintagel, but none of the nobles of the court dared take it up until Tristan begged to be allowed to defend the honor of Cornwall. Mark hesitated, for he loved Tristan well, and did not want to lose such a fine knight in the flower of his youth. But Tristan persisted, and finally Mark relented. Morholt agreed that he would meet Tristan in battle on the morrow, on St Sampson's Isle.

At the appointed time, Morholt and Tristan sailed to the island, both well-armed and each alone in his own boat. The knights saluted one another, and their battle commenced. Such a fight had never been seen before in either Cornwall or Ireland, and doubtless such a fight has never been seen since. Both knights struck mighty blows upon shields, and parried mighty blows with their blades, and the din of it was like the sound of a hundred smiths all fast at their work.

On shore, King Mark and his court anxiously awaited news of the victor, as did the Irish nobles. Hour by hour no word came from St

Sampson's Isle, until the vespers-bell rang. Then one of Mark's courtiers pointed out to sea and shouted, "Look!"

There on the horizon was the sail of Morholt's boat, and the boat of Tristan nowhere to be seen. Cornishmen and Irishmen alike barely dared breathe waiting to see who it was at the helm of that boat. Soon enough it came into the harbor, with Tristan proudly standing in the bows and Morholt lying mortally wounded by the mast. Nobles rushed to pull the boat to shore. Tristan jumped out and showed his sword to the Irishmen: a piece of it was broken off near the tip of the blade.

Tristan said, "Men of Ireland! Your knight fought well and bravely, but in the end the victory was to Cornwall. See here my sword: the piece that is missing you will find lodged in your champion's head. That piece of my sword is the tribute of Cornwall. Take it therefore to your king in Ireland."

Tristan then returned to the castle of Tintagel, crowds cheering his victory while bells rang in all the churches of the city. Tristan smiled and accepted the thanks and praise of his countrymen, but when he finally reached the court and the crowds were shut outside the gate, he crumpled into the arms of King Mark, senseless with utter weariness and the wounds he had received.

The Irishmen for their part took up the body of Morholt and returned to their own land. They sorrowed greatly, for not only had Morholt had great strength of arms, but he was also much beloved by the king and queen and all their court. When they arrived, they gave Morholt over into the care of his sister, the queen, and her daughter, Iseult. Both women were well skilled in the healing arts, and had often tended Morholt and other knights of their household when they returned wounded from battle. But they could not mend such a fatal wound, and soon Morholt was dead, with the fragment of Tristan's blade still lodged in his head. Then the queen and Iseult grieved heavily for the death of their kinsman, and when they were done with their weeping, Iseult went to the body of Morholt and drew forth the piece of Tristan's sword, which she set in a secret place for safekeeping. And from that day forth, Iseult set her heart against Tristan, and vowed vengeance upon him for the death of her uncle.

But neither was Tristan quickly healed of his hurts, for Morholt had struck him with a poisoned lance. The wound festered, despite the ministrations of the best doctors in all Cornwall. Finally Tristan knew that his death was not far off. He begged Mark to have a boat prepared for him, for he wished to be placed in it along with his harp and then pushed out to sea, where he might die in peace, for on the sea had he come to Cornwall those many years ago. For many days, the king refused this request, but soon even Mark saw that Tristan was dying, and so had the boat readied. Mark, Gorvenal, and the Seneschal Dinas, who also loved Tristan well, set him in his boat with his harp. They pushed him out into the retreating tide, where they watched until the little craft floated beyond their sight.

For many days, Tristan floated on the waves in his little boat. He played his harp and sang to keep himself company, and one day this sound came to the ears of some fishermen. It was a strange and haunting song, for Tristan's voice was weak and he could not sing or play for more than a few moments together. The fishermen followed the sound of the music, and when they came upon Tristan they took him into their own craft, where he closed his eyes and scarcely seemed to breathe. The fishermen sailed as quickly as they could for the harbor, for they saw that Tristan was gravely wounded and likely to die. Once ashore in their own country, they bore Tristan to the lady of the castle that was nearby, for she was known far and wide as a healer.

Tristan was brought to a chamber and put into a soft, clean bed, and the lady tended him well. His festering wound soon closed and healed, and when his fever had abated he came to himself and found a beautiful lady with long golden hair sitting by his bedside.

"If it please my lady," said Tristan, "tell me who you are and what place this is."

"This is the castle of Whitehaven," said the lady, "and I am Iseult, the daughter of the king of Ireland."

Then Tristan understood the grave danger he was in, for surely the Irishmen would have no love for the knight who had bested their finest champion and deprived them of rich tribute.

Then the lady spoke. "I have told you my name," she said. "Now favor me with yours."

"My name is Tramtris," he said, knowing that his true name would likely mean the death of him. "I had undertaken a journey to Spain to learn what I could of the harpers there when pirates beset our ship. They wounded me, as you see. I managed to escape, but my companions all perished when their ship sank."

Now, the Lady Iseult had never seen Tristan before, so she had no reason to believe his story false. Tristan spent many days at the court of Whitehaven, and although there he saw many of the nobles who had come to Cornwall with Morholt, none recognized him, so ravaged was he by the illness brought on by his wound.

Under Iseult's care, Tristan soon regained his former strength. And one night, when he deemed the time right, he fled the castle and made his way back to Cornwall, where he was received with joy by King Mark and all the court.

While King Mark and the people of Cornwall loved Tristan well, four nobles there were who envied Tristan his beauty and prowess, and the trust he had of King Mark. And the names of these four were Andret, Guenelon, Gondoit, and Denoalen. It came to their ears that King Mark, who was both unwed and childless, intended to make Tristan his heir, rather than choosing from among the nobles. Therefore the four went to the king, demanding that he take to himself some noble wife, else they would band together and assail Tintagel until Mark was overthrown. Even so, Mark was steadfast, saying that he would have none other than his own dear nephew sit on the throne of Cornwall.

Tristan for his part liked it not, for he knew the nobles deemed that he served Mark not out of love, but that he should gain the throne after Mark's death. Feeling the wound to his honor, Tristan went to Mark and said that he agreed with the nobles, and that if needs must he would leave Cornwall, unless the king were to take to himself a wife and thereby produce a rightful heir. At this Mark finally bowed to the demands of his court, and said that they would be answered after the space of forty days, although he himself despaired of finding a noble bride both agreeable to himself and also acceptable to his court.

One day, while Mark sat at the window thinking on how to find himself a bride, he saw two little birds flitting about, arguing over which of them should have the thing that one clutched in its beak. As they quarreled, the one let the thing fall. It glittered and shone as it fell, golden in the sunlight, so Mark put his hand out the window to catch it. When he had it in his hand, he saw that it was a single, long, golden hair.

Mark took the hair and showed it to his court. "My lords," he said, "I have found who I shall have for my bride. Find for me the woman from whose head this came, and her I will wed."

At this the nobles fell silent, for they knew that Mark was mocking them by this challenge. The four who had first counselled him to marry muttered to each other that Tristan must be the author of the trick, and they looked darkly at him. Tristan knew what they did, so he stood in the middle of the hall and said, "My liege, I beg of you the right to undertake the quest to find the Lady of the Golden Hair. And I vow not to return to Tintagel but with that lady." For Tristan had bethought him of Iseult, daughter of the king of Ireland and her long, fair hair.

King Mark had no choice but to grant this request, so Tristan summoned Gorvenal and a hundred good knights and sailed with them to Ireland. There Tristan and his knights set about pretending to be merchants, while awaiting a chance that would let them bring the Lady Iseult back with them to Cornwall.

One evening, as Tristan and his companions dined in a tavern, the sound of a great wailing roar floated down from the hills and through the air of the town. Tristan asked the landlord what sound that was, for neither he nor any of his friends had ever heard anything so fearsome, and it made even their brave blood run cold.

"That is the voice of the dragon," said the landlord. "Betimes it comes down from its den in the mountains and threatens to burn the town and lay the lands about waste unless we give to it a young maiden. When it roars thus, we know we have until the next evening to choose a maiden to be its prize.

"A score of knights and more have tried already to kill it, but none have come back alive, and more's the pity, for the king himself has said that whoever slays the beast shall have his daughter Iseult to be his bride, and she is the most beautiful woman in all the world. Ah, me," sighed the landlord, who was a grizzled man and shaped like one of his own beer barrels, "were I but twenty years younger and three stone lighter, I myself might even chance that quest, for the Lady Iseult is like none other."

It was then that Tristan knew what he must do. First he asked a question or two more, that he might learn the way to the dragon's lair, but without disclosing his intent. Then he and his companions thanked the landlord for his tale and for the meal. They paid their fare, and then returned to their ship as though they planned to spend the night there, as was their custom. But instead of going to their rest, they helped arm Tristan in secret, and when the harbor and the town at last were all fast asleep, they mounted him on his horse and away he rode to meet the dragon.

On the way to the beast's lair, Tristan saw five armed men come galloping down the road towards him. He hailed them and asked whether he was on the right road to find the dragon. They pulled up their mounts, and one of them said, "That you are, but if you were a wiser man, you would turn around this instant. For that beast surely comes straight from the mouth of Hell itself."

Then the five put spurs to their horses and were away with great speed. Tristan resumed his journey, and soon came into the domain of the dragon. Once the beast had snuffed the scent of Tristan's horse, it came barreling out of its den, nostrils streaming smoke. It was as long as the great hall in the castle Tintagel, with claws red as blood and long and sharp as scythes, and a great maw full of teeth like the tusks of an elephant but sharper than any sword. Also it was covered in great, gleaming scales all over its back and legs, and its great serpent's eyes glowed with a malevolent green light.

Putting his lance in rest, Tristan spurred his charger directly at the dragon. The great steed leapt into battle with a good will, for he was as courageous as his master. Just as Tristan's lance struck the side of the dragon and was shivered into splinters, the monster let out a gout of flame from its mouth. Tristan held off the flames from his own body with his shield, but it was not sufficient also to protect his steadfast friend. The horse crumpled to the ground, dead on the instant. Tristan jumped aside as his mount fell, and drew his sword. He darted to and fro, dodging the dragon's teeth and claws and flaming fire and the lashings of its mighty tail, but though he landed many blows, none could pierce the scales of the beast. Then Tristan darted under the dragon's body and stabbed upwards. His blade found a soft, unprotected space in the dragon's breast, and his blade went straight into the beast's heart. With a deafening scream and a last burst of flame, the dragon coiled in its death throes. It shuddered a final time and was still.

Then Tristan took his sword and cut out the dragon's tongue. He put it inside his armor next to his skin for safekeeping but did not think about the poisonous venom that was in it. Tristan staggered and fell, where he lay like one dead.

While Tristan was fighting the dragon, the five men he had passed on the road stopped at a tavern where they talked among themselves of the knight who had gone where they dared not, and wondered how he had fared. The one who had spoken to Tristan was the Seneschal of Ireland, and a right coward, but he was the leader of that little band. He said to his fellows, "Let us go and see what became of that knight we met on the road. Mayhap we will find something to our own advantage."

So the Seneschal and his companions went back to the dragon's lair, and when they arrived they saw that the beast lay dead and Tristan also slain beside it, or so they thought. So the Seneschal took his sword and cut off the dragon's head, thinking that he would thus have the Lady Iseult for his prize. When the Seneschal showed the head to the king, the king wondered how a man of so little prowess could have slain such a great beast, but he had no choice but to keep his word, and so said that the fair Iseult should wed the Seneschal, but only after the court had judged the rightness of his claim.

Iseult herself was shamed that she would be made to marry a man of little courage and conniving ways, so she called for her palfrey and set out for the dragon's lair, along with her faithful squire, Perinis, and Brangien, her maid. At the beast's den they found the headless body of the dragon and the burned body of a horse, but looking upon its saddle and arms knew that the steed was not that of the Seneschal. Casting about them, they soon chanced upon Tristan, still lying as though dead on the grass. They put Tristan onto Perinis's horse and brought him back to the castle, where Iseult gave him into the care of her mother. When her servants removed Tristan's armor, they found the dragon's tongue, and the queen knew that the venom of it was the cause of Tristan's swoon. She gave him a physic for it, and soon he came to himself.

The queen told Tristan of the Seneschal's deed, and of Iseult's horror at being promised to a knave and a coward. Tristan vowed that he would defend his own honor, and that of Iseult, if the queen could but heal him of his hurts. The queen agreed, gladly, then went to tell her daughter. Iseult wished to know more of this strange knight, so she went to where his arms had been placed. She drew the sword out of its sheath, and there she saw the notch in the blade, which exactly fitted the bit of steel she had taken from the head of Morholt. At this, she fell into a rage, and sword in hand she strode into the chamber where Tristan lay, still weak from the dragon's venom. Iseult held the sword at his breast saying, "I know who you are. You are Tristan of Lyonesse, who slew the knight Morholt, my uncle and a good man. Tell me why I should not now have my vengeance on you."

"Lady," said Tristan, "kill me if you must, for I owe you my life twice over. I was the harper you saved, who came to Ireland in a little boat and grievously wounded, and now a you have saved me from the dragon's venom. But before you avenge your uncle I ask you: did I not slay Morholt in fair combat? Did he not act as champion for Ireland as I did for Cornwall? And did I not also slay the dragon for you? So take then my life, for it is yours, but do this knowing what it is you do, and who it is you slay."

Iseult held the sword still at his breast, but now she was troubled in her heart. She said, "Why then would you come here, since you have set yourself at enmity with Ireland? Why then would you take me unwilling to a far country where I am a stranger, but to punish me and my father and my people?"

Then Tristan told to her the story of the birds and the fair golden hair, and that it was for this that he came to Ireland, to find such a lady, although he did not then say who had sent him or why. And Iseult found herself well answered. She lowered the sword, and there made peace with Tristan.

When the day came for the Seneschal to prove his claim, the king found his hall filled not only with his own courtiers but with a hundred strange knights, all dressed in fine raiment and girt with good swords, for Iseult had sent Perinis to Tristan's ship to give his companions word that they were to array themselves as befit their station and come to the court at the appointed time. There in front of the court, the Seneschal told a tale of how he had slain the dragon, and produced its head as evidence of his prowess and victory. Then the king said, "Is there anyone who would gainsay the claim of the Seneschal?"

For a long moment there was silence in the hall. Then Iseult stepped forward and said, "Noble father, there is one knight here who would gainsay him, and he is none other than the knight who did slay the dragon indeed. But before he comes before you to make his claim, I first ask that you pardon any wrongs he may have done you in the past, whatever they may be."

The king readily agreed. Then Iseult brought Tristan into the hall, and when she did so, the hundred strange knights bowed to him, so that all might know that this was their lord. Some of the Irish knights recognized him, saying that this was none other than the knight who had slain Morholt. A few drew their swords and would have done battle right then and there, but Iseult cried out, "My lord king! You have given your word to pardon this man all his wrongs. Make good now on your promise."

The king ordered his knights to sheathe their swords, and he said that all was forgiven of Tristan, for the king was a man of his word. Then he said to Tristan, "What say you of the Seneschal's claim, and of the reason for your presence here in our kingdom?"

"My lords," said Tristan, "it is true that I slew Morholt. But you fail in courtesy when you think to punish me for that deed: I did battle with him, but only after Morholt came to Cornwall and threw down his challenge at your behest. I stand before you now having repaid the debt of that loss, for truly it is I who slew the dragon. This I did not for myself, but on behalf of King Mark of Cornwall, that he might wed the fair Iseult and by this union thus put an end to all grievances between our two countries. I and the hundred Cornish knights who stand here do swear solemnly that this is our errand, and that we will ever be faithful to Iseult as our lady queen."

Then the king and the lords of Ireland said that they were well answered. And so the king received of Tristan his vow to convey Iseult safely to the land of Cornwall and to King Mark. When all had been made ready, Tristan and his companions took ship for Tintagel, with the Lady Iseult and her maid and squire among them as honored guests, and other servants to do for the lady as she might require.

Now, before Iseult had taken ship for Cornwall, her mother prepared a love philtre, put it in a stoppered flask, and gave it into the keeping of Brangien, telling her to pour it out for Iseult and Mark on their wedding night as though she were giving them a drink of wine, but to keep the flask safely hidden until then, for the philtre had the power to make the two who drank of it love one another with the deepest of loves for the rest of their days. Brangien vowed that she would do as the queen commanded, and so hid the flask among the goods taken into the ship.

The ship sailed towards Cornwall with fair winds, but soon they found themselves becalmed near a little island. The sailors bent themselves to the oars and beached the ship, thinking that all might take their ease on land while they awaited a freshening breeze. All disembarked then, save the Lady Iseult, who stayed on board, sorrowing that she must go to a strange country to be wed to a man she did not know.

Tristan went back to the ship to see what he might do to ease Iseult's grief. The day was hot, and Tristan asked whether the lady might like somewhat to drink. She said she did, so the little serving-girl who was with Iseult went below to see whether she might find some refreshment. Looking about through the hold, the girl found the flask that the queen had prepared. Thinking that the flask held cool wine, she brought it above to her lady, with two beakers, and poured it out for them. Tristan toasted the lady's health, and then they both drank.

It was then that Brangien returned to the ship and saw them both standing there, gazing at one another transfixed. Also she saw the empty flask nearby and knew that the pair had drunk the love-philtre. "Alas!" she cried. "That was no common wine you have drunk, but death."

Tristan knew that Brangien spoke true, for he knew that he loved Iseult more than his own life itself, and that thereby he had betrayed his king, whom he loved like a father. Iseult for her part found her sorrow abated. Within her she felt only love for the handsome knight of Lyonesse, and her hatred of him and of her betrothed husband banished entire. And there on the deck of the ship Tristan and Iseult pledged their love to one another, but Brangien despaired. Telling her friends that their love was but the effect of the potion brewed by Iseult's mother was of no avail: the lady and the knight were in the thrall of love, and vassals of that love they would remain, whether they willed it or not.

When they arrived at Tintagel, King Mark came out to greet Iseult with great courtesy. He welcomed her joyfully to his court, and thanked Tristan and his knights for their courage and steadfastness. Some days later, the wedding of Iseult and Mark took place with great ceremony in the castle chapel. But on the wedding night, Brangien it was who shared Mark's bed, taking the place of her mistress in the dark without Mark's knowledge, for Brangien felt the weight of guilt for Tristan and Iseult having drunk the philtre, and also she did not want to see such a pure love sullied.

Although Iseult was well loved by Mark and by all his court, and although she lacked for nothing in raiment or food or occupation befitting a lady, she could not be happy, for the one she truly loved she could never have. Daily she loved Tristan with all her soul, and daily she sorrowed and feared over it, for she might show that love to no one without imperiling both herself and her beloved. But always Iseult showed her love for Tristan, in glances or in small signs of friendship, nor could he stay his own gestures of love towards her, although these were but moments quickly stolen with the constant hope that they had not been noticed.

The fears of Tristan and his lady were well founded, for the four envious nobles who had first demanded that Mark be wed saw the signs of love between the pair. This they thought to use against Tristan and Mark alike, by poisoning the king's love for his queen and turning him against the nephew he cherished so dearly. The four therefore begged an audience of the king, and told him that Tristan loved the Lady Iseult, and that he had betrayed the trust of his liege lord thereby. Mark refused to hear them, saying that he would yet trust Tristan, who had been ever loyal and who had defended him and the realm of Cornwall with his body against both the knight Morholt and a dragon.

Despite Mark's stout defense of Tristan, an evil seed of doubt had been planted in the breast of the king, and he began to watch Tristan to see whether there were any signs of the love of which he had been told. Mark tired of this ere long, for although he saw the affection between the pair he could find no reason to think theirs was anything but a fond friendship, nor that they had betrayed him in any wise. Nevertheless, the doubt remained, until finally the king could bear it no longer. He called Tristan to himself and told him of the rumors spread by the nobles. "I do not think you have betrayed me," Mark said to Tristan, "but nevertheless I think it best that you remove yourself from my court, both for the ease of my own mind and to stay the foul gossip against your honor and that of my queen."

Tristan sorrowed to hear these words, but he obeyed his lord without protest. Taking only his squire Gorvenal with him, he left the castle Tintagel that very day. He could not bring himself to go far: finding lodgings for himself and Gorvenal in Tintagel town, he there bided his time in hopes that Mark would relent and take him back into his service. And there he found a trial sorer than anything he had endured, more painful even than his combat with Morholt, and more trying to his courage even than his battle with the dragon, for he might not catch even a glimpse of the Lady Iseult by day or by night.

Iseult suffered grievously also. For it was her part to feign love for King Mark, and to lie by his side each night as his wife though she loved another. Iseult no longer had even the quick stolen glances nor the courtly speech she had exchanged with Tristan when she could, and so she pined for him and began to waste away.

Brangien saw this, and knew that if Iseult could not see Tristan she would die. Brangien sought out where Tristan had gone, and found him in his lodgings in the town, where he likewise had begun to wither. Brangien told Tristan to come to the castle orchard and stand under a certain pine, where he should throw chips of wood into the spring that ran past the pine when he wished to see Iseult, for the stream ran through the women's quarters in the castle. This Tristan did, and betimes he and Iseult would meet in the orchard, then part and return to their own abodes before they could be discovered. And in this wise did the health and joy of both return.

King Mark was well pleased that his queen had regained her former vigor, though little did he know the cause thereof. The four evil lords saw this also, and their cunning hearts suspected the reason. Therefore they sent for a magician they knew, to seek his help in discovering how it was that Iseult and Tristan met one another still. The magician cast a spell and saw thereby how Tristan and Iseult were meeting in the orchard. The evil lords brought the magician back to the castle, where he told King Mark that he was yet betrayed by the lovers, and how to lie in wait for them so as to catch them in their disgrace.

That night, King Mark went into the orchard taking with him his bow and also the magician, to see the truth of his claim. Mark hid himself in the pine tree where the spring was, and bade the magician hide himself also. Mark saw Tristan put the chips of wood into the spring as was his wont, and soon the Lady Iseult came through the trees towards him. Mark nocked an arrow to the string, thinking to slay Tristan at the first sign of betrayal. Tristan heard the sound and knew they were being watched. But he could neither stir nor cry out to the Lady Iseult for fear that the bowman might slay her.

Even in the gloom, Iseult could see Tristan's distress in the way he stood. She looked about her, thinking also that mayhap they had been discovered. When saw the shadow of King Mark in the waters of the spring, she knew what she must do, and could only hope that Tristan would understand her design.

"O Sir Tristan," she said, "why have you called me hither? It is not meet that you should do this, as well you know. You have asked many times before and I have never answered, but I am come tonight in the hopes that your pleas will cease thereafter."

"My lady," said Tristan, "it is true that I have asked many times, but I have done so only to discover whether you know why it is King Mark has turned himself against me, for I know of no fault I have committed that might anger him so. I come to beg your aid, for surely he will listen to his queen."

Iseult replied, "Do you not know that the king thinks you have betrayed him with me? And I who have only ever loved he who first pledged love to men. Were the king to know of my coming to you, both our lives would be forfeit."

Then Iseult turned and began to walk back to the castle.

"Lady!" cried Tristan, "In God's name, I beg you: plead to the king for me, for I have done him no wrong."

Iseult turned and said, "The Lord God knows you to be innocent, even if the king does not. Be content therefore."

Then she passed among the trees and out of sight. Mark watched her go, and saw that Tristan made no move to follow, but turned about and left the orchard. The magician saw this also, and so he fled Cornwall lest the king think he had played him false and so kill him. But Mark returned to the castle, and on the morrow sent word that he had pardoned Tristan, saying that he knew the rumors were lies, and that Tristan was once more welcome at court.

The four envious nobles saw this and their hatred of Tristan redoubled. Again they tried to poison the mind of the king, but he would not hear them. Again and again they approached Mark with their complaints, and finally the king's resolve failed. He agreed to allow the magician another trial. This time, the magician told Mark to send Tristan on an errand far from Tintagel, for surely Tristan would not be able to resist speaking to the queen before he left, and this would be evidence of the love he bore for her. Mark ordered it done as the magician said.

Tristan arose before dawn to take the message. The whole castle seemed still to be asleep, so Tristan thought it safe to say a farewell to the queen before he left. He went to her chamber, and when he opened the door he saw that a trap had been laid for him: fine flour was scattered on the floor between the door and Iseult's bed, the work of the magician. Thinking to foil the trap, Tristan made a great leap between the door and the bed. But he also had been wounded earlier that day in a boar hunt. Tristan's leap made the wound bleed afresh, and so drops of blood there were scattered in a trail between the door and the queen's bed, but Tristan did not feel it and so noticed it not.

The magician had followed Tristan secretly, and when he saw him go into Iseult's chamber raised the alarm. Mark and the four nobles rushed into the room to find Tristan standing there, the blood from his wound giving sure proof of his guilt. The nobles rushed upon Tristan and took him prisoner, and the queen as well, and Mark said to them, "I see now that your guilt was not a mere rumor. You shall die for this."

Tristan begged to be allowed to prove his innocence and that of the queen by test of arms, but the king would not hear of it. He locked them in cells in the dungeon, and on the morrow prepared a pyre on which to burn the lovers. When the people of Tintagel found out what the king intended, they cried that he was a false king who burned the accused without even a trial. But the king's heart was now so sorely aggrieved that he would not hear them, and called for Tristan to be taken to his doom.

Now, between the dungeon and the place where Mark had made the pyre there was a chantry standing on the edge of a cliff. As Tristan was taken past the chantry, he begged his guards to be allowed to go within and say a last prayer before he died. "For there is but one door," said Tristan, "and you are armed but I am not; surely I could not leave without your knowing it, nor could I fight my way free of you."

The guards agreed to this request. They cut from Tristan his bonds that he might more easily say his prayers, and let him into the chantry. Tristan made straight for the window behind the altar, for below it was a sheer drop onto the beach below, and he thought to take his own life thus rather than be burned as a common criminal. The young knight burst through the window and plummeted towards the earth, but as he did so the wind caught his cloak and slowed his fall so that he was neither killed nor badly hurt. There he found Gorvenal waiting for him with a horse, for the squire had seen Tristan go into the chantry, and reading what was in his friend's mind had thought to help him escape. And so together Tristan and Gorvenal went to a place where they might lie hidden while they waited for news of what had befallen Iseult.

When Mark heard that Tristan had escaped, his wrath redoubled. He ordered Iseult brought forth straight away and burned. Now, a company of lepers had come to see the burning, and no sooner had Iseult been brought before the king than the leader of them, a man called Ivan, shouted out, "My lord, if you would punish the queen more surely, send her to live with us. By fire she dies but once, but in our company her torment will be the longer." For Ivan was a cruel man, and jealous of the beautiful queen, and he hoped to make her his own slave.

Mark thought on this for a moment, and then agreed to Ivan's plan. He ordered the queen handed her over to the lepers, who bore her away with them. Soon enough, the gang of lepers approached the place where Tristan and Gorvenal lay hid. Seeing his beloved so roughly handled, Tristan sprang into the road and cried out to them to stop. Goaded by Ivan, the lepers took up their staves and crutches and advanced on Tristan, thinking to kill him where he stood. And they would have succeeded had Tristan been alone, for although he could have killed them all in a trice even without his sword, he could not bring himself to strike such pitiable creatures even with his fists.

Gorvenal it was who came to the rescue, swinging a stout branch of oak and buffeting away the lepers. Those he did not strike took flight, but Gorvenal did not pursue them. Rather he gathered to him Tristan and Iseult and after loosing her bonds together they went into the woods of Morois. Gorvenal gave to Tristan a bow and some arrows, and also his sword, then bade the lovers farewell, saying that he would tell no man where they were but would come to the woods from time to time to see how they fared.

And so Tristan and Iseult lived in the woods, making rude huts for their shelter and eating such food as the forest provided. Although they soon became gaunt with hunger and their clothes mere tatters, yet the lovers were content, for they were together and there was none to gainsay them. In such bliss as this they lived, until one day a woodsman by chance found Tristan and his lady asleep inside their hut, with Tristan's naked sword between them. The woodsman rode at once to King Mark and told him where Tristan and the queen might be found, for the king had offered a rich reward to the one who would bring him this news.

Mark then went into the forest with the woodsman, and when they were near the place where Tristan and Iseult lay, the king bade the woodsman begone and went on alone. Mark drew his sword, thinking to slay the lovers. But when Mark saw them, he wondered at their beauty despite their tattered clothes and gaunt faces. Also he saw that they slept with a naked blade between them, and thus he knew that their love had been chaste all along. Mark sheathed his sword, then stepped quietly up to the hut where he gently took Tristan's blade from between the knight and the queen and left his own in its stead. He took a royal ring from his finger, and placed it on the hand of the queen. Mark then withdrew as silently as he had come, and returned to Tintagel.

So deep was her sleep that Iseult did not wake, but she dreamed that Mark had come to her, and told Tristan of this when she woke. When they saw the ring, and that Tristan's sword was missing and the king's in its place, they knew that Iseult had dreamed true. Fearing the king's wrath, Tristan and Iseult fled farther into the depths of the forest.

Tristan and Iseult took thought together of what they might do, so they sought out the hermit who lived in the forest, and bade him write a letter to the king. In the letter, they said that Tristan would bring Iseult to the court if they but had safe conduct, and that there he would offer battle for his honor and for that of Iseult. And if he were defeated, then the king might burn him, but if he were victorious, the king must take back Iseult and either take Tristan back into service, or else he would depart for a far country and serve another king there. If Mark made no answer, Tristan would bring her back to Ireland where she might live in honor among her own people.

Mark read Tristan's terms to his nobles, who counselled the king to take back Iseult and let Tristan go away to a far country. Then King Mark called out, "Is any here who accuses Sir Tristan?"

And there was silence, for none of the nobles wished to meet Tristan in the lists.

Mark therefore sent word that Iseult would be taken back but that Tristan must leave Cornwall forever, and that in three days he would meet them at the ford of a certain river for Iseult to be returned to him. Knowing that they must soon part, Iseult gave to Tristan her ring as a token, saying that if ever he had need of her he should send the ring and she would do as he asked. Tristan for his part gave Iseult his hunting-hound to be her companion and a reminder of his love for her.

On the appointed day, Tristan led Iseult to the ford, and she was wearing fresh raiment bought for her by the hermit that she might not go before the king and his nobles clad as a beggar. There Tristan stood and said, "Behold, I bring to you Iseult, as I promised. I ask once more whether any man will give battle that I may prove my honor."

And none answered him.

Then Tristan and Iseult made their farewells. Iseult went back to the castle with the king, and Tristan made ready to leave Cornwall. But before he went, he hid in the hut of a woodsman who had befriended them betimes, to see whether Iseult was treated well at the court.

But the evil nobles still were unsatisfied with Tristan's disgrace. They counselled the king to put the queen through an ordeal by iron, to prove her innocence. This filled Mark with rage, and he banished them from the kingdom. When he returned to his chamber, he found Iseult there. She asked him, "Why is my lord so angered?"

Then Mark told her what the nobles had demanded, and said, "But you need not fear, for I have rid us of them, and I know you to be faithful."

But Iseult replied, "Let me undergo that ordeal, that my name be cleared for ever, and let your banished nobles also attend that they might see this with their own eyes. But invite King Arthur and his nobles to the trial also, for the lords of Cornwall wish me ill, but Arthur's witness others will believe."

Iseult therefore sent her squire Perinis to Tristan secretly, telling him to disguise himself as a poor pilgrim, that he might witness the trial in secret and safely.

On the appointed day, King Mark and the lords of Cornwall met with King Arthur and his nobles in a field where the trial was to take place. Tristan came also, disguised as a pilgrim, that he might see what befell. A brazier had been set there, full of hot coals, and a bar of iron placed within, for Iseult was to take the hot iron in her bare hands, and if she were innocent, God would protect her and she would not be harmed. Iseult came forward, dressed simply in a shift of white. After saying a prayer with the priest, she swore an oath that no man save her own rightful husband had ever held her in his arms. Then she went to the brazier and took from it the bar of iron in her bare hands. She walked nine steps with it, then cast it from her. She turned to Mark and the assembled lords and showed them her hands and arms, and lo, they remained fresh and unmarked. All praised God and vowed that no longer would Iseult's honor be doubted.

Tristan also witnessed the trial, and when he saw that Iseult's honor had been vindicated, he knew it was time for him to leave Cornwall. Therefore he took up his arms and went with Gorvenal from kingdom to kingdom, serving each lord but a little while, for his heart could never be at rest without Iseult. For two years he lived thus, until he came to Brittany, where he helped Hoel, the duke of that land, rid himself of an evil baron who was laying the country waste. There Tristan tarried a while, and became boon companions with Hoel's son, Kaherdin. After a time, Kaherdin said to his father, "Tristan is a knight like none other, and would make a fine husband for my sister. I beg leave to offer her to him."

Hoel agreed, so Kaherdin went to Tristan and said that his sister, who also was named Iseult, would be his wife, were Tristan willing, and Tristan said he was. But on the wedding night, as Tristan was undressing, the ring that Iseult, queen of Cornwall, had given him fell out of the sleeve where he always kept it, and he regretted having wed.

In Cornwall, Iseult for her part pined for Tristan, for she knew he had gone far away, and never did he once send word to her of how he fared. She knew nothing of how the years had passed for him until one day a visiting nobleman named Kariado came to her and tried to woo her. She spurned him, and so he said, "Well might you pine for your fair knight, for Tristan is wed to Iseult of Brittany, the daughter of a duke."

Then Kariado departed, never to return, but Iseult's sorrow grew the greater.

Now, although Tristan had wed another, his thought ever was for Iseult of Cornwall alone. So one day he disguised himself by throwing beggar's rags over his own clothing, then left Hoel's castle secretly and sought out a ship that might take him to Cornwall. After many days and nights at sea, the ship finally put in at Tintagel harbor, where Tristan roamed about as a beggar, his ear ever open for news of the Lady Iseult. Finally he heard that she was indeed at Tintagel castle, as was the king and all his court. Then Tristan devised a plan by which he might see the queen without being discovered. Changing clothes with a rough fisherman, Tristan cut his long hair and shaved it down nearly to his scalp. Then he brewed a potion that would darken his skin, and he cut a club of oak from a nearby tree. Thus disguised, he went to the castle gate and feigned that he was a fool come to entertain the king and the lords of the castle.

Tristan pranced and prattled before the court, and all laughed heartily and well, all but for Iseult, for the fool listed to them the deeds that Tristan had done, claiming them for himself, and while all thought him merely a raving madman, Iseult was wounded to the core, for she thought the fool was mocking the man she loved most. After the feast, Tristan stayed in the hall, alone, until Brangien chanced to pass through, along with the Lady Iseult. Tristan went to them, and said things that were known only to himself and to Iseult, and finally she knew him to be her beloved. For three days did Tristan hop about and ape the courtiers in the guise of the fool, and for three nights did he go secretly to the Lady Iseult. But after that time Tristan knew he must leave, for the courtiers were becoming suspicious of the attentions paid between the lady and the fool.

And so Tristan returned to Brittany, where he served well Duke Hoel, until one day he was ambushed by an enemy and his side pierced by a poisoned lance. Tristan knew that this was surely the death of him, so he called Kaherdin to himself and poured out all the story of his love for Iseult of Cornwall, thinking that none could hear him. Except Iseult that was his wife did hear, and she grew angry, and plotted her vengeance against Tristan.

At Tristan's behest, Kaherdin took the ring Iseult had given him to Cornwall, to bid the Lady Iseult to come to Brittany to say a last farewell to Tristan. Kaherdin was to take with him two sails: one white, if Iseult were with him, and one black, if she were not. Daily would Tristan watch the horizon, and would know thereby whether his beloved were come to him. When Iseult heard Kaherdin's tale, she went with him gladly, but rough seas and a violent storm pushed their ship off their course, and by the time they were come near to the harbor, white sail aloft, Tristan was too weak to look out the window any longer. It was then that Iseult of Brittany had her revenge, for when Tristan asked whether there was any news of Kaherdin's return, she said there was. And when Tristan asked after the color of the sail, she said, "Why, my lord, it is black as night."

At this, Tristan's heart broke indeed, and breathing the name of his beloved, he died. When the ship came into harbor, they found the whole city in mourning. Iseult asked one of the nobles who had come to greet the ship what was the cause of their sorrow, and he said, "Lady, we mourn for the greatest knight in all the world. Tristan of Lyonesse is dead."

Then Iseult went up to the castle, and came into the chamber of Tristan, where the other Iseult was weeping over his dead body, and with remorse for her deed. "Lady," said Iseult of Cornwall, "do you step aside, for ever have I loved him, longer even than you."

Iseult of Brittany stood aside while Iseult of Cornwall kissed Tristan on the eyes and the brow, and then on the lips. Then she laid herself down beside her beloved and also breathed her last. Hearing of the deaths of Tristan and Iseult, Mark caused fine coffins to be made for them. He came to Brittany, and bore their bodies back to Cornwall, where he had them entombed in that very chantry from which Tristan had made his leap. One night a briar grew from Tristan's tomb, and wound its way across the chantry until it came to rest on the tomb of Iseult. And those who tended the chantry cut the briar back, but every night it grew back. When Mark was told of this, he forbade the caretakers to cut the briar any more.

And thus ends the tale of the love between Tristan and Iseult.

Pronunciation Guide

Modern Celtic languages fall into two broad groups: Brythonic Gaelic (also known as P-Celtic) and Goedelic Gaelic (also known as Q-Celtic). The Brythonic branch includes Breton, Welsh, and Cornish. Of these, only Breton and Welsh continue to have native speakers. Cornish became extinct as a first language in the eighteenth century, but was revived in the early twentieth. The Goedelic branch includes Manx and the various dialects of Irish and Scottish Gaelic. The latter two continue to be a first language for a small percentage of the populations in those countries. The last native speaker of Manx died in 1974, but Manx has continued to be spoken as a second language on the Isle of Man.

The following standards will be used for sounds in the pronunciation guide:

ai = as in fair

ay = as in shy

ah = as in far

ee = as in feet

eh = as in yet

ih = as in it

oh = as in no

oo = as in food

ow = as in down

oy = as in boy

uh = as in under

g = as in good, never as in giant

<u>ch</u> = ch as in loch

tch = ch as in child

th = voiceless th as in thin

<u>th</u> = voiced th as in they

Irish Names and Words

ilbhe (AIL-vyeh):	Foster daughter of Bodb Derg
lba (AHL-bah):	Scotland
mergin (AH-mehr-gin):	Foster-father of Cuchulainn
obh (AIV):	Foster-daughter of Bodb Derg and first wife of Lir
odh (AI<u>TH</u>	Son of Aobh and Lir, twin brother of Fionnula
oife (EE-feh):	Second wife of Lir
odb Derg (BOHV DAIRG):	King of the Tuatha De Danann
reg (BREGG):	Plain between the Liffey and Boyne Rivers in County Meath, eastern Ireland
ricriu (BRIK-roo):	One of the nobles of Ulster under King Conchobor
rugh na Boinne (BROO nah OYN):	Site of the Boyne Valley Tombs, County Meath, eastern Ireland
arraig na Ron (KAIR-egg nah	Rock of the Seals

OHN):

athbad (CAH-hbahd):	Druid of the court of Conchobor
onall (KONN-all):	One of the nobles of Ulster under King Conchobor
onchobor (KONN-uh-cover):	King of Ulster and foster-father of Cuchulainn
onn (KONN):	Child of Aobh and Lir
onnacht (KON-ahcht):	Province of central western Ireland
u (KOO):	Irish Gaelic word for "hound"
uchulainn (KOO-CHUH-lin):	"Hound of Culann"; superhuman hero of Ulster
ulann (KOO-lown):	Smith whose guard dog is destroyed by Cuchulainn
agda (DAHG-duh):	Ancient Celtic deity; one of the Tuatha De Danann and father of Bodb Derg
eichtine (DAICH-tin-eh):	Sister of Conchobor
eoch (DAI-och):	Wife of Lairgnen, King of Ireland
iarmuid (DEER-mud):	Irish warrior and character in the Fenian Cycle story "The Pursuit of Diarmuid and Grainne"
dmonn (ED-mon):	Place in Ireland mentioned in the story of the birth of Cuchulainn
main Macha (EH-vin MAH-ah):	Seat of the court of Conchobor in Ulster; also known simply as "Emain"
ergus (FAIR-gus):	1. One of the nobles of Ulster

	under King Conchobor 2. Son of Bodb Derg and one of the Tuatha De Danann
achra (FEE-ah-<u>ch</u>ra):	Son of Aobh and Lir; twin brother of Conn
dchell (FEED-chell):	Ancient Irish board game that may have been something like chess
nn mac Cumhaill (FINN MAK OO-uhl):	Ancient Irish hero of the Fenian Cycle of myth
nnchaem (FINN-uh-chaym):	Sister of Conchobor and foster-mother of Cuchulainn
onnula (FINN-oo-lah):	Daughter of Aobh and Lir; twin sister of Aodh
ollamain (FALL-uh-vin):	Son of Conchobor
adhar (GAY-ar):	Irish Gaelic word for "dog"
rainne (GRAH-nyeh):	Woman betrothed to Finn mac Cumhaill in the story "The Pursuit of Diarmuid and Grainne"
arith (IM-rih):	Name of the stronghold of Amergin and Finnchaem of Ulster
is Gluaire N-ish GLOO-air-eh):	Island off the coast of County Mayo, western Ireland
rus Domnann (IHR-us DOV-own):	Irish place name
aegire (LAY-gir-eh):	One of the nobles of Ulster under King Conchobor

airgnen (LAIRG-nen):	A king of Ireland
ir (LEER):	One of the Tuatha De Danann; originally Lir may have been a sea-god
och Dairbhreach (LOCH DAIR-n-vrach):	"Lake of the Oaks": lake in County Westmeath, Ireland
ug (LOOG):	Ancient Celtic deity; probably a solar god, associated with warriors
ug mac Ethnenn (LOOG mak H-hnen):	An avatar of Lug
il (MEEL):	Leader of a group that invaded Ireland in the pseudo-history "Book of the Takings of Ireland"
ochaomhog (MOH-chay-vohg):	Priest who built a church in Inis Gluaire
orann (MOHR-own):	Judge at the court of Conchobor
urtheimne (MOOR-hev-neh):	Place in northeastern Ireland, County Louth
etanta (SHAI-tan-tah):	The childhood name of Cuchulainn
dhe (SHEE):	The "good people" or fairy folk; the Tuatha De after the coming of Christianity
dhe Fionnachaidh (SHEE NN-ah-chai):	One of the homes of the Tuatha De Danann before the coming of Christianity
iab Fuait (SLEE-av FOO-itch):	Peak in the Fews Mountains, County Armagh, Ireland

uth na Maoile (SROO nah [EEL-yeh):	The Straits of Moyle; strait between northern Ireland and Scotland
ialdam mac Roich (SOO-al-im mak ROY<u>CH</u>):	Husband of Deichtine and third father of Cuchulainn
ain Bo Cuailgne (TAYN BOH OO-al-nyeh):	Irish epic hero story of the war between Ulster and Connacht
iatha De Danann (TOO-ah-ha \I DAH-nan):	"Children of the Goddess Danu"; race of supernatural beings who come to Ireland in the pseudo-history "Book of the Takings of Ireland"; may originally have been the Celtic gods

Welsh Names and Words

The pronunciation guide is the same as above, with the addition of the Welsh "rh" and "ll." These sounds do not exist in English.

ll = a voiceless "l"; nearest analogue using English pronunciation is to think of it as a sort of "lth" or "thl" sound, depending on where it falls in the word

rh = a voiceless "r"; nearest analogue using English pronunciation is as "hr"

Anlawdd (AHN-low<u>th</u>):	Grandfather of Culhwch; father of Goleuddydd
Annwfn (Ah-NOO-vin):	Otherworldly realm
Arawn (ah-ROWN):	Otherworldly king of Annwfn
Arberth (AHR-bairth):	Court of Pwyll, prince of Dyfed

Bedwyr (BED-weer):	One of the knights of King Arthur
Branwen (BRAN-wen):	Main character in the second branch of the Mabinogion; sister of Manawydan
Cantref (KAHN-trev):	Welsh word for county
Celli Weg (KEL-thee WEGG):	Place in Cornwall mentioned in the Mabinogion
Celyddon (kell-<u>ITH</u>-on):	Grandfather of Culhwch; father of Cilydd
Ceredigion (KAIR-eh-DIG-ee-ahn):	Region of western Wales along the central coast
Cilydd (KILL-i<u>th</u>):	Father of Culhwch
Clud (CLID):	Father of Gwawl
Culhwch (KILL-hooch):	Welsh hero, possibly an analogue to the pig-god Moccus
Custennin (kiss-TEN-nin):	Shepherd and father of Goreu
Cwm Cerwyn (KOOM KAIR-win):	Place in Wales mentioned in the Mabinogion
Cyledyr Wyllt (kill-EH-deer WITHLT):	One of the knights of King Arthur
Cynddelig Cyfarwydd (kin-THEH-lig kih-VAHR-wi<u>th</u>):	One of the knights of King Arthur
Doged (DOH-ged):	King who is slain and whose wife is taken to be wife to Cilydd after the death of Goleuddydd
Drych Ail Cybdar (DRICH AIL KIB-dahr):	One of the three fastest men in King Arthur's realm

Dyfed (DUH-ved):	Place name in the Mabinogion
Esgair Oerfel (ESS-geyer OHR-vell):	Place in Ireland mentioned in the Mabinogion
Glyn Ystun (GLINN ISS-tin):	Place in Wales mentioned in the Mabinogion
Goleuddydd (go-LAI-<u>th</u>i<u>th</u>):	Mother of Culhwch
Goreu (GOHR-ai):	Son of Custennin
Gorsedd Arberth (GOAR-se<u>th</u> AHR-bairth):	Welsh place name; hill near the court of Pwyll
Grugyn Gwrych Eraint (GRIG-in GOOR-ich AIR-eyent)	One of the sons of the boar Twrch Trwyth
Gwalchmai mab Gwyar (GWAHLCH-meye mahb GOO-yahr):	One of the knights of King Arthur
Gwawl (GOO-owl):	Rival of Pwyll for the hand of Rhiannon
Gwent Is Coed (GWENT iss COYD):	Place name in the Mabinogion; seat of the nobleman Teyrnon Twrf Liant
Gwri Wallt Euryn (GOO-ree WALTHT AI-rin):	Childhood name of Pryderi, son of Pwyll and Rhiannon, and foster-son of Teyrnon
Gwyn (GWIN):	Character in the story of Culhwch and Olwen
Gwyrhyr Gwstad Ieithoedd (GOOR-heer GOO-stahd ee-YAI-thoy<u>th</u>):	One of the knights of King Arthur
Hafgan (HAHV-gahn):	Rival of Arawn for lands in Annwfn

Hafren (HAHV-ren):	River in Wales
Hyfaidd Hen (HUH-veth HEN):	"Old Hyfaidd"; Father of Rhiannon
Kai (KEYE):	One of the knights of King Arthur
Llyr (THLEER):	Father of Branwen and Manawydan; Welsh analogue of the Irish Lir
Mabinogion (mah-bi-NOH-gyon):	Collection of Welsh myths and legends
Mabon (MAH-bohn):	One of the knights of King Arthur
Manawydan (mah-NAH-wih-dan):	Main character in the third branch of the Mabinogion; brother of Branwen
Math (MAHTH):	Main character in the fourth branch of the Mabinogion
Mathonwy (MAHTH-on-wee):	Father of Math
Menw (MEN-oo):	One of the knights of King Arthur
Modron (MOH-drohn):	Father of Mabon
Nudd (NITH):	Father of Gwyn
Olwen (OHL-wen):	Bride of Culhwch and daughter of Ysbaddaden Pencawr
Porth Clais (POHRTH KLEYESS):	Place in Wales mentioned in the Mabinogion
Pryderi (prih-DAIR-ee):	Son of Pwyll and Rhiannon
Prydwen (PRID-wen):	The name of King Arthur's ship

Pwyll (POO-ilth):	Lord of Dyfed; friend of Arawn, husband of Rhiannon, father of Pryderi
Teirgwaedd (TAIR-gweye<u>th</u>):	Father of Menw
Teyrnon Twrf Liant (TAI-eer-non TOORV LEE-ahnt):	Nobleman who takes in the foundling son of Pwyll and Rhiannon
Twrch Trwyth (TOORCH TROO-with):	A king who was changed into a giant boar
Ysbaddaden Pencawr (ISS-bah-THAH-den pen-KOWR):	Chief of the giants and father of Olwen
Ystrad Tywi (UH-strahd TUH-wee):	One of the cantrefs mentioned in the Mabinogion
Ystrad Yw (uh-STRAHD EE-oo):	Place in Wales mentioned in the Mabinogion

Other Names and Words

Pronunciation of personal names from "The Drowned City of Ys" and "The Romance of Tristan and Iseult" are mostly given according to Old French standards, except for "Tintagel," which has a Modern English pronunciation, and "Menez-Hom," which is Breton.

The pronunciation guide is the same as the one given above, with the exception of the front-rounded u, which does not exist in Irish or English.

ü = front-rounded u as in Modern French cru

Andret (AHN-dret):	One of the four evil nobles of Cornwall

Baie de Douarnenez (BAI de DOO-ahr-neh-NEHZ):	Bay along the Brittany coast
Baie de Trepasses (BAI de tre-PASS-eh):	Bay along the Brittany coast
Blanchefleur (blahnsh-FLOOR):	Mother of Tristan; wife of Rivalen; sister of Mark
Brangien (BRAN-zhee-en):	Iseult's maid
Corentin (KOH-ren-tin):	Hermit who aids Gradlon; later Bishop of Cornouaille
Cornouaille (kor-noo-AY):	Region of Brittany
Dahut (dah-HÜT):	Daughter of King Gradlon of Cornouaille
Denoalen (deh-NOH-ah-len):	One of the four evil nobles of Cornwall
Dinas (DEE-nass):	Seneschal of Cornwall and friend of Tristan
Epona (eh-POH-nah):	Celtic horse goddess
Gondoit (GON-doh-eet):	One of the four evil nobles of Cornwall
Gorvenal (GOHR-ve-nahl):	Squire to Tristan
Gradlon (GRAHD-lon):	King of Cornouaille
Guenelon (GWEN-eh-lon):	One of the four evil nobles of Cornwall
Guenole (gwen-oh-LAI):	Abbot of the monastery of Landevennec
Hoel (HOH-el):	Duke of Brittany; father of Iseult of Brittany and Kaherdin; father-in-law of

	Tristan
Iseult (ee-SOOLT):	1. Wife of King Mark of Cornwall; lover of Tristan 2. Daughter of Hoel and wife of Tristan
Kaherdin (KAH-her-din):	Son of Hoel and companion of Tristan
Kariado (kah-ree-AH-do):	Nobleman who woos Iseult of Cornwall
Korrigan (KOHR-rih-gan):	An Otherworldly creature in Breton myth
Landevennec (lahn-de-VEN-nek):	Monastery in Brittany
Lyonesse (lee-oh-NESS):	Country in France in Arthurian legend

Check out this book.

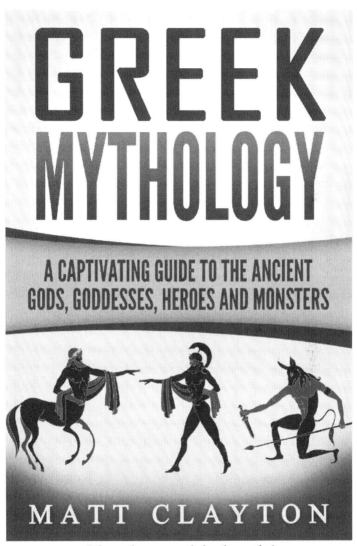

Check out this book!

BIBLIOGRAPHY

Augusta, Lady Gregory. *Cuchulain of Muirthemne: The Story of the Men of the Red Branch of Ulster*. London: J. Murray, 1902.

Bedier, Joseph. *The Romance of Tristan and Iseult*. Trans. Hilaire Belloc. New York: Dodd, Mead & Co., 1917.

Cross, Tom Peete and Clark Harris Slover, eds. *Ancient Irish Tales*. Totowa: Barnes & Noble Books, 1936.

Davies, Sioned, trans. *The Mabinogion*. Oxford: Oxford University Press, 2007.

Delaney, Frank. *Legends of the Celts*. New York: Sterling Publishing, Inc., 1991.

Eddy, Steve and Claire Hamilton. *Celtic Myths*. Chicago: Contemporary Books, 2001.

Ford, Patrick, trans and ed. *The Mabinogi and Other Medieval Welsh Tales*. Berkeley: University of California Press, 1977.

Guest, Lady Charlotte. *The Mabinogion: From the Welsh of the* Llyfr coch o Hergest *(The Red Book of Hergest) in the Library of Jesus College, Oxford*. London: Quaritch, 1877.

Hodges, Margaret. *The Other World: Myths of the Celts*. New York: Farrar, Straus and Giroux, 1973.

Kinsella, Thomas, trans. *The Tain: Translated from the Irish Epic Tain Bo Cuailnge*. Oxford: Oxford University Press, 1969.

Macalister, R. A. Stewart. Lebor gabala Erenn: *The Book of the Taking of Ireland.* Vols. 2-5. Dublin: Irish Texts Society, 1939-1941, 1956.

Mac Cana, Proinsias. *Celtic Mythology*. London: Hamlyn Publishing Group, Ltd., 1970.

Markale, Jean. *The Epics of Celtic Ireland: Ancient Tales of Mystery and Magic*. Rochester, VT: Inner Traditions, 2000.

O'Connor, Ulick. *Irish Tales and Sagas*. Dublin: Town House and Country House, 1996.

Price, Bill. *Celtic Myths*. Harpenden: Pocket Essentials, 2008.

Rolleston, Thomas William. *Myths and Legends of the Celtic Race*. London: Harrap, 1911.

Squire, Charles. *The Mythology of Ancient Britain and Ireland*. London: A. Constable, 1906.

Zaczek, Iain. *Chronicles of the Celts*. New York: Sterling Publishing, Inc., 1997.

Free Bonus from Captivating History (Available for a Limited time)

Hi History Lovers!

Now you have a chance to join our exclusive history list so you can get your first history ebook for free as well as discounts and a potential to get more history books for free! Simply visit the link below to join.

Captivatinghistory.com/ebook

Also, make sure to follow us on:

Twitter: @Captivhistory

Facebook: Captivating History:@captivatinghistory

Made in the USA
Columbia, SC
18 May 2019